DEMENTIA

A Journey Through A Different Life

By

Stewart Nosky

This book is a work of non-fiction. Names and places have been changed to protect the privacy of all individuals. The events and situations are true.

© 2003 by Stewart Nosky. All rights reserved.

ISBN: 1-4107-5569-X (e-book)
ISBN: 1-4107-5568-1 (Paperback)

This book is printed on acid free paper.

1st Books - rev. 06/06/03

ACKNOWLEDGMENTS

I must acknowledge my mother, Margaret, for inspiring the writing of this book. I thank my wife Jan, without whom I could never have cared for my mother nor have written and finished this book.

CONTENTS

INTRODUCTION

This book is being written to tell the story of one woman's struggle with Dementia and how it affected the lives of her family and friends. It is not an in depth "how to" or a highly researched documentation on people with Dementia. Rather, it is a back ground story of a middle class woman who was a wife and a mother, but succumbed to the mental instability that comes with Dementia. Along the way I will try to show things that could help someone who may be involved in a situation where you are faced with caring for a parent that needs special care. As you read this book, you will see the different cycles and situations that a person with this disease goes through and also how a son or daughter might cope with the various phases. The attempt here is to give an accounting of the way a person evolves through this disease. Obviously, this is one person's story and is different from someone else's situation. However, in my dealings with my mother through her many phases, I have found that working with and meeting other people and patients, there is a constant thread of similarity in almost every situation I have encountered. I believe that some of the situations that were encountered in seeing my mother through this phase of her life and what had to be accomplished to get her by and keep her alive can be helpful to families about to walk down this path.

CHAPTER ONE

EARLY ON

I'm not sure exactly when things started to go wrong for my mother even as I look back. I can remember over a period of years when she was in her seventies that I believe she was thinking some things that weren't true. She seemed to really think, on a couple of occasions, that some people had stolen from her, but suffice to say, the situations were not very believable. No one I know that was involved ever thought anything about my mother having a bonafide mental condition of any kind. My mother was a strong competent person with everything seemingly under control. After all she had been a Registered Nurse, a Women's Club president and an elected official. What does this have to do with anything? Not much except to say she has been capable of paying attention to detail and had organizational abilities.

Nothing happened with my mother's personality that was significant throughout her seventies. My parents had been living in a small town in North Carolina as retirees. They purchased a smaller house, which they had redecorated more to their liking. My wife and I would visit them in North

1

Carolina a couple of times a year, especially on Christmas or Thanksgiving. We lived in Pennsylvania so we weren't tuned in on the every day happenings of their life, but would talk to them about once a week. When we did visit, some of these old fears did crop up occasionally. I remember one time my mother told us that a lady she had known for years, who had been a women's club buddy, had stolen some old record albums from her cabinet right out of her living room. Things you have to remember are that as a family member, this is hard to dispute. You usually do not know what your parents have accumulated and you lose track after a period of time. I did know that some of the record albums supposedly missing had been given to me years ago. Did she really have some of the albums she thought she had? I don't know. At this time none of us ever thought these symptoms were signs of anything medically wrong. Only now can I look back and see that in her case, this was the start of her present condition. Was there something that could have been done at that time? Possibly, but as I said, we did not think of her as having a real medical problem. What did we think was wrong? We thought she just had an occasional personality quirk and was becoming more intolerable as she got older. Keep in mind, feelings my mother had like this were not that frequent. As you get to know Dementia patients, you will find that they really don't see anything wrong at all. To suggest any treatment would be extremely fruitless even if, as a family member, you were able to recognize a problem early on.

In this period of her life, my mother had no problem getting through the daily grind. She was a good cook and kept house well. My parents seemed to have friends and regularly did various things with them, such as dinner at each other's house and at restaurants in the town.

After living in North Carolina for a few years, my father had gotten ill and was getting worse. He had a couple of strokes, but Mother had no problem in caring for him. This was due to her previous nursing skills being put to use. But, after a few years, my dad wasn't able to keep going and finally passed away.

My mother moved back to Pennsylvania, but my wife and I were still unable to visit as often as we'd like, except for special occasions. We had moved from Pennsylvania to Alabama. My mother seemed to settle down fairly well and life was as normal as it could be. She was living alone in an apartment and seemed to be more lonesome as time went by. When we would visit we could see that she was becoming more paranoid about various things. For example, she thought her drapes had been stolen by her landlord and had been given to a friend that lived a few miles away. We would drive by the friend's house just so I could look at the drapes. Obviously I tried to brush it off. My wife and I were still not aware of how Dementia develops. Ten to fifteen years ago actions like these were thought to be senile. Keep in mind she still functioned well most of the time, especially doing the essential things in life. My mother was now eighty years of age but looked as if she was in her seventies. As I mentioned she was getting lonely and had expressed a desire to move down south with us.

CHAPTER TWO

A TURNING POINT

My wife and I really thought the time was coming that she needed to be near family. My brother was in Michigan and the weather there did not really appeal to her. We brought my mother down to Alabama for a visit and one of the things we were going to do was look at some apartments for senior citizens. The places we had in mind are places that you have to function on your own. We visited many places in our area and my mother sort of settled on one that she thought suited her. There is always a waiting list so you are never sure of when an apartment will be available. After visiting, Mother went back home until we might hear something. I would call the apartment manager occasionally to see if anything had become available. Finally an apartment became available and we were off and running to relocate Mother. This was quite an undertaking. After all it was eight hundred miles between the two cities. For this task we had to enlist the services of my brother and his wife. The move was going to be a task. Mother had a one bed room apartment but it was full of furniture she had from another larger house. To find a starting point was going to be difficult. My wife and I were staying with her parents who lived fifteen minutes away. This made any trips back and forth to my mother's place a little more tolerable. My brother and his wife came down from Michigan to help with the moving. They stayed with her parents who also lived a short distance away. We had to get all the items that were not going to be kept sorted out and taken to the Goodwill charity. Of course Mother had to identify everything that was selected and decide if she wanted it or not. It was hard for her to decide whether she wanted a lot of these items. Too many things were being saved which meant the apartment was not being emptied as fast as we would have liked. We decided that we would need a plan to deal with this. Many things Mother had were never going to be used again. We knew she would also agree, but to show her everything just slowed the whole process. My brother and I would take these types of items and drive them to Goodwill without her seeing them. This seems sneaky, but we only did this with broken items, something that wouldn't work or something there was no chance she would use. This plan seemed to speed things up. Mother was happy to be moving and going with us. She was never one to think ahead very much but she thought being with her son was probably the best thing to do. Besides, Mother liked to travel a lot. This move would be exciting if not only for the sake of traveling.

My wife and I had flown to Pittsburgh because of the move and to be able to drive Mother to Alabama in her own car. The drive is a long one and usually uneventful. We make sure to make enough stops to keep my mother comfortable. Bathroom stops are obviously essential for an older person. We did take two days to make the trip. We stopped earlier than usual due to my mother getting tired. When I reserved the room, I got two rooms that adjoined each other. This enabled us to keep an eye on her. Of course at bedtime we closed the doors for privacy, but slightly opened them after everyone had gotten settled. Mother was capable of showering and dressing herself, but there was always that fear of her falling. We made the rest of the trip the next day. Our destination was our house due to my mother staying with us until we could get her moved into her place. The moving truck would be here in a couple of days.

The furniture came and we were under way getting Mother moved. There were boxes and boxes piled all over the apartment. Our first duty was to set up the bedroom and living area furniture. Then we had the kitchen to contend with. We decided to take our time and do the job right the first time. No one had extra time to redo anything. This was a nice senior place to live and we wanted her to be happy.

This type of senior living requires no assistance. A person has to function on his or her own.

Complexes of this type do offer the following: The mail is distributed to their mailbox. Security is offered in the form of entrances being either locked all the time or during certain times of the day. Admittance is gained by the use of a key, or an alarm button notifying the attendant to let you in. Transportation can be arranged from a local service operating through the residence. If you have your own automobile, which most people do at this level, a specific spot is designated for you to park. Residences of this type are usually one and two bedrooms with kitchens. Pricing on apartments of this type can have a varied range. Depending on what part of the country you live in, the range can be between four hundred to fifteen hundred per month. It's best to try to find an apartment development that is subsidized by the government. These are sponsored by HUD, Housing and Urban Development. The senior apartments subsidized by this group are nice, well maintained and clean. Management is usually good because HUD regulates the rent and generally watches over them.

Mother settled into her apartment and seemed to be moderately content. She was the type of person that never really was completely happy. I guess the grass was always greener somewhere else. At first she started to make some friends and participate in a few activities. As she got older, she seemed to not want to make friends. Activities were posted on a calendar day by day for a month at a time. Exercise classes, card games, crafts and even dancing is offered as a means to keep the residents active. We tried to get her to participate in things that would interest her. Years ago Mother was an avid Bridge player. We kept after her to go down to the recreation room and join the Bridge players. After a short while Mother started to Play Bridge. At first it was okay although she said that her group was a little clannish. There is no telling what the level of play is like at their age so when something goes wrong no one knows who is to blame. They would fight over rules, playing too fast, or talking too much. Finally my mother quit the Bridge group. She just didn't get along with people like she did in her early years. This was due in part to her distrust of people. This distrust seemed to be for no good reason and was probably due to a mild paranoia that was approaching.

So, life went along fairly normal for my mother. She still had her own car and drove it anywhere she wanted to go. Even though she was in her mid-eighties, she seemed fit enough mentally and physically to be able to drive. As time progressed there were areas of high traffic that we would rather she did not drive in, but when this was mentioned she said she really did not see why she shouldn't drive anywhere she chose. Mother was coping with daily life with help from my wife and me. I would bring her over to the house for dinner about every Sunday. We would try to have things that she liked to eat, that way she would look forward to coming over. Some times it was tough getting Mother over for supper. She liked staying at home in her apartment. At least when she was at our house, we knew she had one good meal that week. Mother was doing most of her grocery shopping. The store was not far away and in a light traffic area. She could still manage gathering and checking out her groceries and getting them home into her apartment with no problem. Sometimes I would take my mother shopping to make it easier on her. She would push the shopping cart while I picked out what she wanted. It got so that we would go up and down the same aisles because she would eat the same things every week. Actually it cut down the shopping time having only certain aisles to visit. Mother had particular cookies, cranberry juice and other favorites that were a must every week. She and I would stop at the frozen dinner case and pick out enough dinners for about a week. Of course, there were only a handful of dinners that she liked. Consequently we had to double up on a lot of varieties to be able to buy seven or eight. These dinners are not the best food for a person's diet especially for the high salt content. But, my mother had a very normal blood pressure, even compared with someone half her age. Some of the dinners have about half the salt of the others. I think these dinners are all right for older people if they don't have a problem that might be worsened by something in the food. My mother doesn't really want to cook a regular meal for herself anymore. At least with frozen dinners and some dessert she will have something to eat. I usually count her dinners in her freezer and at the end of the week I will know hopefully how many dinners she has eaten. I say hopefully because there is always a chance some dinners are thrown out. You really have to watch closely when dealing with an older person if you are responsible for their eating habits. Dealing with frozen dinners is a very easy way for them to have food that is close to something they might make instead of taking a chance with cooking on a stove. Using a microwave is much safer and easier.

My mother's driving was looking as though something was going to change. She had previously been involved in a couple of fender benders. They were very minor accidents and did not require any repairs to either automobile. This was very fortunate, but we were afraid of what the next encounter might bring. Based on these accidents we told Mother not to drive too far and to stay off the more heavily traveled streets. This did not go over well with her because she didn't think any of the accidents were her fault. We looked at the causes as slow reflexes and not fully looking where she was going. I had decided to ride along with my mother the next time we had to go somewhere. Up until now, unless it was grocery shopping, I was volunteering to take Mother everywhere she had to go. The next time She had to go to the bank, I said, " I will go with you." I came over to her place and got in the car with Mother in the driver's seat. She backed the car out of the parking space and proceeded out of the main parking area to the road. As we turned on to the road I noticed we were almost in the middle instead of our lane. I said something and Mother straightened the car right away. It appeared she was unsure and nervous about driving. I kept taking Mother places after this, except grocery shopping which was only a street over from her place. Not too long after this incident my mother was complaining that she didn't drive enough any more. I tried to explain that I thought she shouldn't drive much any more, if at all. This did not go over well, so I told her that I would come over, since she hadn't driven much, and take a drive with her. Reluctantly she agreed. In a day or so I drove over to her place to go shopping. She asked me to back the car out of the parking space. I did and then let her in the driver's seat. What followed was shocking to say the least. Mother had a blank look on her face and I said, "Put the car in gear and let's go." She hadn't positioned her power seat, which was the first thing she did. Mother sat in the seat and did not remember how to start out driving her own car. I asked her what was wrong and she said, " I don't remember how to do this." This whole scene was more of a disaster than it sounds. The panic look, the look of despair and total fear was hard to believe. I told her to move over and I would drive. Mother didn't have much to say as we drove to the store. I think she was realizing that her driving days were over. Fortunately Mother had not been driving at all lately, not even grocery shopping. We did not have to take her keys or disconnect the battery, although we thought hard about both. I just didn't think she would try to drive again, and I was right. The car just sat in her spot and we would occasionally discuss selling it.

This episode, along with some others that I will discuss was making us take notice of her mental health. As I have said, Mother did not want to make friends. But, she did get to know a couple of ladies on her floor. They would run in and out of each other's apartments sharing their troubles and bits of advice. One lady right across the hall became her "good" friend. My mother and she would bring each other food that they had made or were given. My mother would never eat food prepared by a stranger. I guess it was all thrown away. As I said we were getting concerned about certain things that were happening with Mother. This particular lady across the hall was very friendly. Her name was Gertrude and she was around eighty years of age. Sometimes when Mother was coming over to eat at our house, she would ask, "What should I wear?" I would tell her that as usual the dress was casual. She told me that Gertrude would help her pick something to wear. I was shocked at this revelation and asked how often this happens. She told me it happened only a couple of times. Needless to say we were more and more concerned with each development. Throughout this period Mother was taken to her regular doctor visits and deemed to be in good health for her age. We also were on guard for her physical stability so as not to put her in unnecessary jeopardy. If I had thought there was a reason that would preclude her from living alone, we would have made quick changes. Keep in mind that all older people can fall at any time even though they are very capable of living alone. There was another instance of concern one night when I was talking to her on the phone. We were discussing how to change channels on her remote control. For some reason she said her up and down channel selector would not work. I told her she could change channels by pushing the exact number buttons for the channels she wants to change. She said she wanted to put on channel 9, so I said to push the 9 button and point the remote toward the television. In a few seconds I heard a beep as though someone was pushing the phone buttons. I asked her what she

was doing and she said, " I'm pushing the 9 button."
What Mother was doing was pushing the 9 button
on the telephone. I was able to get her straightened
out fairly quickly, but I was still surprised at what
had happened. The episodes I have discussed and
will discuss in this chapter are not of great
significance on their own, but have substantial
meaning as a group. These incidents happened
infrequently over a period of a few years but became
more frequent in later years. This is the problem of
distinguishing normal old age senility from
Dementia.

Mother had some old dishtowels that were getting
quite worn and developing holes at the ends. She
claimed that someone was coming into her
apartment and cutting them. Basically Mother was
blaming the Resident Manager, whom she did not
like for reasons I will discuss later. Mother was also
missing things. If you remember early on in North
Carolina she was thinking the same thing and that
was years ago. Just about any of her belongings
were subject to scrutiny. Any time she would look
for things to wear or use, usually it meant that we
would hear something such as, "I used to have more
of these than this." Keep in mind Mother was very
coherent, ambulatory and able to keep an orderly
apartment.

Mother was involved in an event that led to her
disliking the Resident Manager. She was walking

from her car in the parking lot of a local retail store. A woman approached her and said she had just won a foreign lottery. She showed my mother the winning ticket, but needed a sum of money for certain fees before she could collect. The lady asked Mother to give her the money now or they could go to Mother's bank and get the money. The deal was that if they split the fees they would also split the prize money, which as I remember was significant. Mother, being suspicious and stubborn, told the lady to get lost and quit following her. I know this happened because she called me from a pay phone just after it occurred. I was alarmed for fear of someone harming her. Mother said the lady was not in sight. I asked her to get the manager or a worker to escort her to her car when she was finished.

A while after this event my mother had decided the manager of her building was the very same person that had accosted her in the parking lot. I didn't think much of it at the time, but it began to gather momentum. Mother started to blame her for most of her problems. This goes back to the cut towels and missing items, which now included underwear and just about anything else. Mother was looking through her phone book for the manager's last name and came to the conclusion that the manager was related to some lawyers in town. This made Mother afraid to confront the manager about anything. She also felt the manager was trying to have her moved out. None of these ideas or feelings Mother had was expressed on a daily basis. They were things that would come up now and then. Some how through a bulletin that is published by her doctor, Mother associated her doctor's wife with her building manager. As I remember, they were to have worked together on a charity committee of some sort. The only way the two people could have been connected was if someone with the same name as the manager was working with the doctor's wife. This led to my mother thinking her building manager would know about any medical treatment she was receiving which would lead to her eviction. So, no matter what happened or what was thought to have happened during this period of time could have been laid on the manager's doorstep according to Mother.

Another situation my mother was involved with was concerning her television. She watched a lot of television between sleeping in her chair and talking on the telephone. One show she liked was called "Hardball," a political information show. I don't know how she got started with this program due to its nature and the fact that the host talks very fast. Somehow Mother thought the host was smiling at her through the television screen. Also they would wave at each other and say hello. She actually showed me this at her place when the program came on. At first my wife and I told her this is impossible.

She agreed but also continued to mention it periodically. These were isolated moments over a long period of time, but were a cause for concern.

We tried to get Mother to go away with us at least once a year to change her scenery. We have a yearly family reunion trip to the beach in North Carolina each August. My wife and I have to start in June to persuade her to go. Every year it is the same story, " I had better not go this year." This was her line each time the subject was brought up. We would have to say, "Everyone wants you to be there, it wouldn't be the same without you." This would go on and on until days before we would have to leave. I can remember talking her into going the night before leaving. I tried every approach, even agreeing with her about staying home. She called back later and thought she should go. This happened even though we had packed her suitcase the day before. One time it was even more bizarre. The morning we were leaving and were to pick her up at 8:00 A. M., Mother called at 7:00 A. M. to say she was not feeling well and couldn't go. She said she had some pains in her chest area. The only thing I could do was to suggest the emergency room. Mother agreed to this and we went to the hospital at 9:00A.M. We checked her in and she was taken right away. Then comes the wait. The doctors run a lot of tests for this type of complaint and there are no shortcuts. It is getting close to noon and the final test was in and the verdict was no heart problems that would have caused the discomfort. What it was, as it always was, her arthritis kicking up again. In this case I also suspect a case of nerves was partly the problem. Actually Mother was satisfied with the doctor's diagnosis. She should have been; it was the same one as other times she had been to the emergency room.

Well, we were able to leave for the trip around 1:00 P. M. which was five hours late. She was a tough person when it came to this kind of adventure. We traveled in a van with the back seats fixed so Mother could lie down for a nap if she wanted to. It was rare that she did because she was so curious about what was going on. Sometimes she would sit on the edge of the back seat and lean forward to talk with us for long periods of time. It wasn't necessary to hurry because there wasn't a strict time frame to adhere to. My wife and I believed that the older the traveler, the more consideration they should have. All of a sudden Mother would get weary and cranky. You need to be prepared for stopping shortly after that. If you are in a hurry traveling, I don't think I would take a person along that is older and needs special care. As I said before in moving Mother down with us, a motel with adjoining rooms is a good idea. It's good to keep close tabs when an older person, in this case a family member, is in unfamiliar surroundings. Really, unless there is car trouble, illness or something else unforeseen, trips like this can be smooth with a little planning. Making the trip comfortable is key.

We would cruise into Nags Head, NC early Sunday afternoon in time to get our condo keys from the Realtor. The next thing we did was to buy the food staples we needed for the first few days. Mother would like pushing the shopping cart up and down the aisles. This would help loosen her up after the long trip. After this chore we would head for the condo. We were usually earlier to arrive than the rest of the family because the first evening's dinner was Mother's. Of course my wife and I would help quite a bit and some of the main courses were brought from home in a cooler. The rest of the families would drift in later in the afternoon. Each family would take a night to prepare dinner. We had two condos, which made it a lot easier for everyone. The dinners would be seafood based due to the fact that it was very fresh and available and everyone liked it in one form or another. We all went out to dinner on the last night there. My mother liked all of the socializing and seemed happy.

Mother had been a beach person for years and we had been coming to this area since I was eleven. We would spend time trying to find old places that we had known to see if they still existed.

Mother was able to walk fairly well and could make her way to the beach with a little help from everyone. She would sit under the umbrella and watch her great-grandsons as they played in the sand. She always loved the beach and was fond of hunting for seashells. At this point in her life, Mother's seashell hunting days were not the same. If the wind were too strong it would knock her over if we weren't careful. Part of the day Mother would spend at the beach and the rest of the day watching television or napping.

We weren't immune to the Dementia problems she was having at home just because we were at the beach. One incident occurred after Mother had gone to sleep. She had her own room and awoke shortly after midnight. I heard her up to the bathroom and made sure I saw her go back to her room. This particular night I went over to see her and she told me someone was trying to get in her room through the outside door that led to the deck area. No matter how hard I tried to explain or show her no one could possibly get in or be in her room, she would not believe me. So, she was up most of the night until she was so tired it didn't matter anymore. This quieted down for the next few nights and we made it past that upsetting period. Generally, Mother was content and having some fun. Just about every night anyone who wanted to play poker would play. The kids would play with adults looking on and helping. My mother was an old Bridge player but also liked poker. She was able to follow cards pretty well but I would sit beside her and make sure she knew what her cards meant.

So, we just do the beach thing, eat too much food, and relax doing anything that comes up. Mother partakes when she feels like getting involved. Time goes by quickly and before you know it's time to leave. We all have a good time at the beach each year and look forward to the next year.

CHAPTER THREE

THE BIG FALL

It was December, 2000 and everyone was looking forward to the holidays. My mother was her usual self, getting along pretty well and not very interested in the holiday festivities. She could decorate her apartment herself with little items. This would take some prodding on our part.

My wife and I took Mother to the clothing store to buy some new things for her to wear for Christmas. She bought quite a few things and was happy trying them on at home. We always had problems getting her to try on her new clothes at the store.

Our Christmas plans were to drive Mother to my brother's home in Michigan and let her spend some time with him. We would go on to my wife's family in Pennsylvania, then return to Michigan for New Years. Everyone was set for these plans and looking forward to them.

Sunday, December 17, 2000, I was to pick up Mother at 3:00 p.m. for supper. I drove to her place and waited out front as usual. Until recently she would come down from her apartment on time. Lately, she has been forgetting appointment times.

Stewart Nosky

I'm waiting in front of her place and it's about ten minutes past three. Not wanting to wait any longer, I went up to her apartment, knocked on the door and then heard the sound no one wants to hear. My mother was crying out "Help me, please help me." My key to her apartment was not on the key ring of the car I was driving. I knocked on the door and said, " I'll be right back!" I ran to the elevator and went to the first floor where the security guard was. I told the guard my mother was crying out inside her apartment and that I did not have a key. We were running to the elevator as we spoke. We got off the elevator at her floor and ran to her door just a short distance away. As soon as we entered we ran to the bedroom where my mother was lying on the floor crying. I told the guard, Margaret, to call 911. I tried to quiet my mother but couldn't. She did not want to get up nor was I going to move her. I put her head on a pillow and tried to make her more comfortable until the emergency vehicle arrived. The emergency people arrived within three to five minutes. Somehow they got her on a stretcher and took her down to the vehicle. I went to pick up my wife and from there we headed for the hospital. This is really the point where you find out what's wrong and what kind of treatment lies ahead. We thought that a leg or hip was fractured by the leg position as she lay on the emergency room bed. My mother was cold and in pain so the nurse gave her pain medicine. A technician finally took her to x-ray. This all took about two hours from the time we arrived. After another long period of time the doctor came in and gave us the diagnosis. The femur bone, which is the largest bone in the body, was broken. This was not good news considering her age (91). Our next step was to see the doctor that was actually going to do the surgery. After an hour or so, the surgeon came by and explained the procedure. It was to be a routine operation; in fact he had done four already that day, before my mother. I guess besides listening to the description of the operation, the most important things you can glean are, will she recover, how long does it take and will she be as good as she was. The doctor said that the reality of it is, that it is a big "hit" to a person of her age and that she may or may not walk again. It all depends on how strong physically and mentally a person is.

The operation only took about an hour, and then Mother was admitted to a room in the hospital. The next day we visited her, not expecting too much. It was a good thing we weren't because she was very sedated and could not respond. The little she was awake was at meal times. No one was able to get her to eat. For the first few days she was not able to feed herself. She was not eating or drinking even for the nurses when they would try to help her to eat. It looked like it was coming to being fed intravenously and after a talk with the doctor, that's what was done.

I guess my approach to most everything is "buyer beware". I wanted to make sure my mother had the best care possible. I think the way the situation is today, with personnel in all walks of life, makes one pay more attention to the service being provided. I know that hospital personnel are supposed to be more professional than most, but I believe that because of personnel shortages and under trained personnel, things can happen that aren't believable. As I said Mother was on intravenous for nourishment and medication. When my wife and I would visit her we would naturally look around to see what was going on that day. It so happens that a male nurse came by to check Mother. I noticed he was a little rough looking around the edges as far as his clothing was concerned. His name tag was a home made job to say the least. I made small talk with him for a while and found out he had just relocated here. As we tried to stay out of his way I noticed that he was changing the intravenous bag that still had some fluid left. For no real reason we asked why it was being changed now. He said they work better at a higher level and since he was there he could change it now. Sounded logical to us. He was having some trouble fitting the new bag on the stand but finally succeeded. We thought we would watch this operation a little longer and noticed the drip rate to be a lot faster than it had been before being adjusted. Then it was adjusted slower and then to a different rate than ever before. I asked him if something was wrong and he stood back a little and squinted at the machine and said, "I have not used this machine before and it takes a little getting used to." Well, that was enough for me. I asked another nurse to check the rate of drip and anything else concerning the machine. Another thing we noticed was that this male nurse was asking every nurse what he or she wanted him to do next. These weren't supervisory nurses. He appeared to be training and training alone with no guidance. I went to find the highest level person on duty at that time and told her my story. Whether she believed me or liked me I didn't know but I never saw that particular male nurse again. The problem with situations like these is, as a layman you can only use common sense to get through something you feel is not right. I could have been wrong about the male nurse, but with someone's life literally hanging in the balance, can you take a chance? Also you are usually paying a premium price for this kind of service. It ought to be premium service.

My mother started to come around and all of a sudden after a few days, she was talking coherently on the telephone to my brother.

Still, she would not eat. Part of the problem was the hospital food and the other aspect was that she just did not want to eat. Unfortunately for Mother, she had an intravenous needle in her right arm and was very weak in her left arm. Of course this is common in older people who are not well. So you might think that institutions would make a real effort to help with feeding patients. In a hospital this is not the case. Nurse's aids deliver the meals and are supposed to help a patient eat. The caveat is the aid cannot stop delivering meals, so the patient doesn't get any immediate help. At least they are supposed to get the meal set up. This means opening sealed items, cutting food if needed and using any additives, sweeteners, etc. A lot of times this is not done. Consequently the patient will not get to eat that meal. If someone comes by to check on something they may realize that none of the food has been eaten. When the patient is fed, the food is too cold and is not edible. I have seen this with my mother and with roommates she has had. There are patients that are on a list that absolutely can make no move towards helping themselves eat. These patients are helped but it is not one hundred percent effective and the timeliness is still wanting. What can the problem be attributed to? I think many things contribute to the problem, such as sloppy management, worker indifference and worker absences. Probably the main deficiency is a planned shortage of workers. This stems from budget restraints and /or reduced access to a meaningful worker pool.

After about one week she looked about as strong as she would be in the hospital. There had been no weight put on the broken leg as yet and she was too weak to do much for herself. We were also paying attention to her mental condition as far as memory loss or any other differences we could observe. Mother did not know exactly why or when she came to the hospital. If I had it to do over again I would stress more often at this time what had happened and when it happened. We were really concerned that Mother would not get beyond this point. She was progressing so slowly that at her age it looked hopeless for any recovery.

This is the time one starts to think about how someone in this state of health is going to be taken care of in the days ahead? How much assistance will a person need. Where can they get the proper care? What is the cost involved and is there any insurance and if there is, how much will it cover? So, now came the time to deal with the reality of where would Mother be cared for. I really think people start wondering about home care first. Of course this route depends on what your resources are. Can you manage from a people and cost standpoint? If there is no insurance or insurance that pays for a short while, care can be difficult. To care for someone at home there has to be a dedicated person that can devote 100 percent of his or her time. With today's work schedules this is very rare. Without any insurance even home care can be costly. Special nurses or therapists visits may be required. I believe it is the rare occasion that someone is cared for at home by a family member. Medicaid insurance is there as a last resort for people without resources. This is government-sponsored insurance when all funds are exhausted and the patient is in an institution.

There are social workers at hospitals that are there just to help you deal with this problem. Our social worker told us that she would find a rehabilitation center for us. The first place that has an opening is the one that is offered. This could be a center that is not as good as you desire for various reasons. You are better off, in the short term, taking the social worker's suggestion because it is a lot of work to find a place yourself that has an immediate opening. It probably can't be done in a timely manner. We went to check out the place our social worker found. We had our fingers crossed and fortunately it was a very nice looking clean place. Talking to the Director of Admissions is the next vital thing to do. He seemed very interested in taking care of Mother. His qualifications for his position were very impressive. He took us on a tour of the facility and it looked as though it would be a good place to put Mother. Actually I'm not sure what we would have done if the facility were really sub par. I guess we were lucky. I believe you could always transfer to another facility and would have more time to locate a better place. Through Medicare and other insurance Mother would be fully covered in the rehabilitation center for 120 days. It is best to check out your own supplemental insurance for the amount of coverage and for any extended coverage. Medicare is pretty standard but other insurance coverage is not. After going through the preliminaries, Mother was transferred to the rehabilitation center. She was weak and her weight was down. We found that, at 91, there is a fine line between life and death when you are in this condition.

CHAPTER FOUR

REHABILITATION

Prior to actually entering the rehabilitation center, you must make sure all the necessary paperwork is completed. This is done with the help of the Director of Admissions.

Patient transfers are done by the local ambulance service. The Hospital arranges the transfer in conjunction with the receiving institution. The family is notified of the patient's departure and arrival dates. The ambulance services that take care of these situations are used to doing this and do a very good job.

After you get settled in the rehabilitation center, department heads come in one by one to talk to the family. In fact the Director of Admissions was the first to come by to welcome Mother. The department heads want to get any pertinent history they can to get a clearer picture of the patient. It's a good idea to spend extra time with the Head Dietitian, the Director of Nursing and the Head of Physical Therapy. The dietitian wanted to know what favorite foods my mother likes and what are her least favorite foods. Also can she eat regularly prepared foods or do they have to be pureed? Should the diet be low fat, sugar free or salt free? Would I be bringing mother's favorite foods to supplement her diet? The Director of Nursing is interested in any medications and allergies that a new patient has. Although this information is sent from the hospital, it is a good idea to go over it with the nurse to make sure there are no errors or omissions. The family member responsible for the care and safety of a patient should write down all medications and monitor them to the best of their ability for adverse reactions or ineffectiveness. If there are any doubts about medications, the charge nurse or doctor should be notified.

The person in charge of the physical therapy department is interested in what happened to the patient and some background information concerning the patient. Again, they have the patient's records, but any information you can supply is helpful. The therapy department has its specific methods for specific medical problems, so they do not deviate very much.

After the initial contact with the department heads, a weekly meeting schedule is posted where families get their pertinent information. The people involved in these meetings can be department designees or the department heads themselves. On meeting day they move from room to room so you have to time your arrival and sometimes wait awhile. If a family member is waiting, the staff holding the meetings will usually defer to the family that is there. Not all patients have family visit them, especially for the meetings. I was able to ask many questions so as to get a baseline each week and see where Mother was heading. These people are very helpful, so it is good to take advantage of these weekly meetings. I would ask each group how they thought Mother was doing. Although they are the experts it doesn't hurt to know what they think and compare it to your thoughts. I would contribute my thoughts about Mother to the staff to get feed back from them. Not that they would not do their best, but I think that knowing family is attending meetings and is interested, keeps them on their toes. I think it is up to the family member to monitor differences in their family member's health at least on a weekly basis.

Therapy was started right away one to two times a day. There is a minimum amount of therapy set per day by Medicare. I was getting reports that the therapy was going very slowly. Mother was afraid to try to stand even with help. Although she wasn't allowed to put weight on the broken leg for two weeks, they wanted her to do as many things as possible to increase strength. It was amazing to see the difference in my mother from the way she was in the hospital. We went from almost no hope of recovery to a feeling that maybe anything is possible. Therapy was to be the key to her recovery and future. I was developing a close rapport with Mother's lead therapist. We were able to sneak in and see Mother during her therapy sessions without her knowing. This was good and bad. The bad part was seeing her in this condition not being able to function. The good part was seeing that she could at least do some of the minimal activities and that she was being treated well. It is unbelievable how much a person, especially elderly, can go down hill after a fall.

Mother was getting stronger from eating better. She did not like the food even though food services tried to give her what she wanted. Because Mother had dentures, her food was pureed which made it look unappetizing. The taste was still the same but my mother was not going to try it. There was a food preference list at the outset that allowed you to specify the cooking format of your food. Obviously no one looked at it. Sometimes she would get sugar free items delivered. I talked to the head dietitian about getting Mother's food changed to a regular diet. It took a few days for the change to take place. Remember to be persistent about everything that you feel merits change.

The doctor thought an appetite enhancer might be of some value. There are various opinions as to whether these medicines work for everyone. He said it could take a couple of weeks to show any improvement. My wife and I thought it was worth a chance since there were no side affects. Mother started taking the medicine in liquid form. At first she was doing all right taking it, but then suddenly she would spit it out and refuse any more. Evidently it has a bitter taste. They decided to use the pill form although supposedly not as effective. The only thing we could do was to feed her the best we could and wait for the medicine to work.

My mother had not been taking any medication on a regular basis except for some aspirin type medicine for arthritis. Her blood pressure and other vitals were good.

It was becoming apparent that Mother's memory was failing, at least the short term memory. Sometimes she even forgot where she was. She had a phone by her bed and I wrote my number on the phone. I would get calls from her at night telling me she didn't know why she was in this place and wanted to come home. The staff referred to this condition as "sundowners syndrome" because it was worse at night. The lapse in memory and confusion is said to worsen in older people after each fall.

Despite Mother's good health, she developed a urinary infection. I guess this was to be expected. No one can pinpoint exactly why this happened. Possibly her condition not being as sanitary as it should be. Also she was not drinking enough fluids. A medicine was prescribed and seemed to work for a while. Part of the problem with this condition in an older person is that they do not realize they have it. There is a burning sensation but it is not always communicated to the doctor or nurse. What I did with my mother was to ask her every day if she had any burning feeling. If she did I would tell the staff. That's about the only way to keep on top of the situation. Not all medicines for this condition work the same for everyone. If you have a tolerance for a certain medicine it may work for a short time. That's what happened with my mother. The doctor had to take a urine culture to find the exact strain so he could give the medicine that fit that strain. After that was done, Mother felt much better. One way to discover that a person has a urinary tract problem is to watch their behavior. If they are tired and sleepy without any energy and a bit irritable, the urinary issue should be investigated.

Two weeks elapsed and Mother was supposed to see the surgeon. He was going to tell us whether she could bear weight on the broken leg. The doctor looked over the x-rays and said she could start weight therapy right away. We had to get a written order from the doctor to give to her therapist. I gave the order to the lead therapist when we took Mother back to the rehabilitation center. By the way, my wife and I took Mother to see her surgeon. There is a shuttle service that's available in most areas. They are very good and safe, and there is no charge for a patient, but family pays a modest fee. Sometimes the shuttle is more convenient depending on the patient's condition.

When my mother got back in therapy, she forgot that the doctor told her to stand on the broken leg. Needless to say the therapists had a problem with that. Mother would tell the therapists that she was not supposed to walk on her bad leg even though the doctor had just given her permission. Her lapse of memory was really going to play a negative roll in her recovery.

The therapy continued slowly. Mother was also getting occupational therapy as well. This was to help her keep her skills as far as dressing, grooming and using the bathroom. This was in preparation for resuming her everyday life. Over the weeks that followed we all worked with Mother to get her to walk at least with a walker. I would try to get her to walk with me in the rehabilitation center's hallways. She was reluctant many times to do this because she felt she should not for many reasons. Mother would forget she had been told to walk on the broken leg, she was afraid and I believe self conscious in the hallway. When a person is able to stand and hold on to a walker, the next step is learning to walk again. A way to do this is to take a strap with a sliding buckle and put it around the waist of the person learning to walk. The straps are available from the therapy department. I put this strap around my mother's waist and held the end of it. It's long enough to allow you to be right beside the walker. If the person wobbles you can steady them quickly pulling on the strap. The therapists would work with Mother during the day and I would work with her at night and weekends. After a few weeks Mother was able to walk alone with a walker. We did feel as though she could not walk with out supervision. During the times she was not in therapy or with me, the attendants would put her back in her wheel chair. When they could they would take her out of her room and put her with other people. If she tired, the attendants would lay her down in her bed for a nap. We did not want her in bed too much due to bedsores or just getting too complacent. Mother did not work well with other people when she was in her wheelchair and put in a recreation room or congregating around the nurse's station. I think it was embarrassing for her to be in this situation. She wasn't accustomed to being on display with a condition that put her less than equal with other people. She couldn't realize that everyone around her was in the same condition or worse. This thinking made her want to stay in her room and not socialize. I would come to visit Mother in her room and sometimes find her out and about. She was happy I was there but wanted to know where I had been. With her memory becoming more forgetful, she did not know the last time I was there.

Being in a rehabilitation center is a hardship for the patient but it can also be a different type of hardship for the family. Visiting with the frequency that is required to make sure things are going right is not easy. We were fortunate that we had just sold our business and had more time to devote to my mother. My wife was an important part of this total picture. She would visit with me most of the time. She would take care of cleaning my mother's clothes, although, the center would do it for a fee. They would lose or misplace many clothing items, so it is better to tell them the family will do the laundry if possible.

Lack of communication is the biggest obstacle you will have to overcome. The people that you deal with are very different and of course have different levels of authority. Besides the therapists who are professional and try to do a good job there are, CNA's, Certified Nurse's Assistants who give the day to day one on one care. This job takes a person who is dedicated, but most are there until something better comes along. The duties can be nerve racking and dirty at times. Usually a CNA is over worked and under paid. Probably a day doesn't go by without someone calling in to report off work. This starts the whole day's cycle off in the hole as far as getting things done. The patient suffers the repercussions. Many times in this setting patients have to be helped with their meals. As I have mentioned before I have seen patients meals delivered to their bedside and watched it sit there and get cold because no one is free to help feed. If you see this you have to call someone.

I'm not sure of the qualifications or testing you need to be a nurse's assistant. I believe a lot of it is on the job training. Fortunately they are only allowed to give custodial care. Most I have encountered are very friendly at least when they are in your presence. Although most are probably friendly most of the time, it's evident that work is not a favorite place to be. The best approach, I believe, is to get to know the people that take care of your family member. Be nice to them and they will treat you and your family member better. If there is a problem that can't be resolved with the nurse's assistant, the first stop should be at the nurse's station. Only talk to the charge nurse on duty. After the complaint is lodged, you have to follow up to see if any action has taken place. A lot of times nothing is done, especially if it has to cross shifts. This is where communication really breaks down. I guess in dealing with the nurses and their assistants, the best approach is to know them, be friendly and follow up on any problems. I hate to say this but, if there is a staff birthday, any special occasion or a holiday, a nice thing to do is to bring in goodies for the staff to eat. It really does have a positive effect on your relationship with the staff.

Stewart Nosky

We continued working with my mother over the next few weeks to get her back to as close to normal as possible. My mother was getting more unsettled as she progressed. We would catch her trying to get up from her wheelchair by herself. One time she fell to the floor. When they called me I thought it was back to square one. Fortunately nothing was broken. One method we found that was somewhat helpful was a chair alarm. This is a battery operated alarm which fits on the chair with a cord attached from it to the patient. If the patient moves forward in the chair too far the cord pulls and sounds the alarm attached to the chair. The fallacy in this is that someone has to be close by to stop any further action by the patient. I happened to drop in for my daily visit about 3:00 p.m. one day and went into Mother's room. I didn't see her in her bed nor did I see her wheelchair. The bathroom door was halfway open so I peeked in and there she was standing, wondering what to do. She had gotten up from her wheelchair to go to the bathroom but was at a loss as how to proceed further. I immediately went in and helped her back into her wheelchair and buzzed for a CNA to help her continue to the bathroom. I guess being there at that time was a stroke of luck, although visiting every day I was bound to run into a situation like this. I reported what had happened to the charge nurse. You can't stop things like this from occurring but a significant problem here that could be discussed was that the chair alarm was not hooked to my mother, probably from the beginning of the day. Of course the charge nurse was sympathetic and would make sure it wouldn't happen again. Probably the reason little would be done is because the flow of information down the chain is not adequate.

Let's discuss the previously mentioned lack of communication from the top down. When you talk to a person in charge, preferably the head or lead person, about a problem or change that should be made, you expect some satisfaction or meeting of the minds to take place. When a solution is reached the charge person is supposed to relay the information down the line. The ways that I am familiar with are direct communication between the head charge person and the supervisors. Another way is by having shift overlap meetings and having the problem addressed there. The first method usually starts with a breakdown between the head charge person and a supervisor due to the timeliness of the information exchange. Time and interest loss starts here. When the supervisor receives his/her directive, he/she has to relay it to the pertinent workers. This is done by word of mouth to the workers that are known to be involved with the particular patient. Needless to say this method lacks a clear and decisive path. The problem is all the directives are given by casual conversation between the responsible parties. If a substitute worker is in place for a few days, then the directive is probably temporary. If the right worker is not given the new directive nothing is gained. The shift overlap method is a more precise way of communicating a change to a patients care. When you talk to a head charge person make sure the new directive is written in the patient's chart. I would always stand around and wait for this to happen or ask if they would write in the chart while I was there. If you are nice about situations like this, people will accommodate you. This chart is always available at the nurse's station involved in the specific patient's care. Each supervisor, nurse and CNA has access to and is required to review it. This is best done on the shift over lap sessions where all levels of caregivers from two shifts are available to talk among themselves and discuss the patient they have in common. Some problems can occur when a caregiver is a substitute, not sure of his/her duties or just late for work. I think this method works well if charts are read and have the needed information in them. Most facilities have a patient chart system that they use. This system works well, but the key is the get the information in the chart initially, unlike the first method described.

Mother had a semi-private room. For a while she was fortunate that there was not a patient available for her room. That did not last long. Mother was not very sociable, as you know. So, when a roommate was brought in, you could see the look on her face as if to say, " What is she doing here"? My mother always made sure her curtain partition was drawn at least halfway to keep them separated. I guess this is not too unusual for a person in her mental state. Part of the reason was fear of something unknown. I remember one roommate Mother had that talked and moaned all through the night. I knew this because Mother told me and, as a back up, one of the CNA'S on night shift related the story to me. It was apparent that Mother was sleepier than usual during the day. She was feeling well and no current signs of urinary infection. I asked Mother if she was sleeping enough through the night and she said again the "old coot" next to her was yelling all night. This is what she sometimes called people twenty years her junior. I went to the charge nurse and she said they were giving this lady a sedative to see what could be done. It didn't look like something that should be waited for so I went to the Director of Admissions and told my story. He said they would look for a room to move my mother. I told him she isn't the problem and is happy and adjusted in her present room. It did have a window on her side. He saw my point and put in for a transfer for the roommate. This seemed to me to be a valid request to do something about the situation. The problem wasn't minor due to the toll it took on Mother's sleep. She had future roommates that had minor quirks but I'm sure Mother had hers, too. It's something you have to adjust to.

Physical and mental abuse of the patients by the assistants is a realistic problem. Obviously this occurs mostly when the family is not around. You get to know the families of other patients on your floor and especially roommate families. We all try to watch out for each other's family member when possible. We know we had one episode of physical abuse involving my mother. Mother's roommate had her family visiting one day while we were not there. We were visiting that evening and this family was still visiting their mother. My wife and I were over on my mother's side of the room when the daughter of Mother's roommate came and asked to speak to me in the hallway. Evidently a male CNA was attending to my mother and was going to put her back in bed for a nap. She had said she did not want go to bed at that time. The male CNA picked up my mother and dropped her on the bed and said, "You're going to bed now." The daughter who was witnessing this said something to the CNA about the treatment but did not receive an answer. I did know the CNA she was telling me about from him taking care of Mother sometimes while I was there. I had my eye on him from the start because he did have a gruff attitude. He would pass this off as his way of getting patients to do things for him. Ironically at the first meeting I had with the Director of Admissions discussing his facility and staff, he brought this particular individual up in his discussion of the CNA's staffing and duties. His view of this fellow was that he was a little terse and gruff on the surface, but it was just his way of dealing with patients and that really he was harmless. As I learned later this was the CNA's own description of himself. Now I know why I thought this was so strange at that first meeting. After the daughter told me what she had seen, I went to the Director of Admissions with the information. I relayed the story and that the culprit was none other than our CNA that we had originally talked about. He made no comment to that statement and I didn't push the issue. I told the director to make sure it doesn't happen again. I knew Mother did not have a long stay left, but it only takes one time for something bad to happen. The director concurred and said that he would take action to get to the bottom of it. We didn't see that fellow in Mother's wing again.

Mother was progressing to a point in her therapy where there didn't appear to be room for significant improvement. The lead therapist was noticing Mother reaching a plateau. She said when this occurs they are required to notify Medicare. Medicare will only pay for therapy when there is room for improvement that will take the patient to another level. It was time that I scheduled a meeting with the therapy department head. Therapy said the best they could do was set a release date for about two to three weeks from now. We talked about Mother's condition affecting her progress. I told the therapy department that her periodic urinary infections and lack of sleep might have something to do with her leveling out. These certainly must be factors they could consider. I wanted Mother to have the longest therapy time possible and still be within Medicare's payment term. Also I asked them to notch up her therapy, especially the occupational type, knowing the release date is near. We didn't think Mother was as ready as necessary to be released. Therapy agreed to work with her more and to push back her release date.

We only had about three weeks to get the transfer worked out and locate Mother a place to live. Facilities of this type also have a social worker on staff. It is their job to facilitate any paperwork and related items for a smooth checkout. The social worker is notified by the front office of any imminent patient change and then they contact the family. The checkout procedure is not very complicated. The family's part is limited except for locating a place to live. The facility obtains doctors' releases, medicine plans and follow up treatment, if any, such as outside therapy.

This is the time to focus on what level of care the patient will need when released. As time went by with my mother we pretty much knew the level of care she would need. Mentally she was forgetful and not able to readily understand everything. Physically she currently needed a walker to get around and that is with assistance if only to be close by. We were wondering if Mother was going to progress any more. In her present condition going back to her unassisted apartment was not an option. She required assistance with her daily living duties. She needed help with getting out of bed, getting dressed, going to the bathroom, preparing meals and most other physical tasks. At this juncture Mother could do all of these things with a little prodding and careful assistance. Home care was not an option. We could not provide the expertise or time it takes to give that care. We resigned ourselves to the fact that Mother needed to be in an assisted living facility. She would get the professional help she had to have. In the back of our minds we were hoping she would progress to a point where she could be back in her independent status. I don't think we really believed this.

We would talk to Mother about leaving the rehabilitation center, especially now at the end of her stay. Prior to this, she would always be asking when was she getting out and going home. About all the information we would give her along the way was the estimate of days left. She didn't remember her apartment, so I don't know what "home" meant. We would tell her she could have help for a while after leaving the center. Now, discharge was imminent and we talked to her more about her next home. I tried to make her understand that she would be in a place that had people who would take care of her. Mother was sort of receptive to this because she indicated at times that she couldn't completely take care of herself. I thought this was clear thinking that was encouraging. The problem was Mother's memory was so short that this would be forgotten in no time.

A few days before Mother's departure we were doing a few things at once. We were in discussions with the social worker, the Director of Admissions, the Head of Therapy, billing and the charge nurses. Also my wife was gathering and sorting clothes to take home. We wanted very little left in her room on the last day.

The social worker wanted the address of Mother's new home. We were able to give her that because we had chosen a place. In the next chapter I will get into choosing a place to live. As I recall there were a few release forms that the social worker had us sign. With the Director of Admissions the discussion was more general, wishing us well, etc. The Head of Therapy wanted to know if she needed to set up any outside therapy at this time, or wait until later. We said we would let her know. She did order an elevated commode chair, a walker with wheels, a bathtub seat and a wheelchair. Medicare paid for all of this except the wheelchair, which was on a rental basis. I didn't know this and at the end of its use you have to pay a nominal fee and return the chair. The other items are yours.

When you have other insurance and Medicare, the billing department just wants verification that all items such as telephone and laundry are paid up.

Finally departure day came. Mother's new place wouldn't be ready until early afternoon. The CNA's were to have Mother dressed and ready to go by noon. We arrived and Mother looked nice and was in a good mood. She was walking by herself with a walker and close supervision. She could use the bathroom alone and get up and down out of a chair alone. There had been amazing progress since her arrival. We spent some time going around visiting the staff and saying goodbye. The nurse's station had our departure packet of paperwork and any medicine that was left. The medicine was bubble packed, which we will get into later. As we left I took a picture of Mother walking out of the facility by herself.

CHAPTER FIVE

CHOOSING A PLACE TO LIVE

As I had stated, home care for us was not an option. What are the options beyond home care? The basic options are assisted living and nursing home care. Obviously independent living is not an option at this point. Recently there has been an upswing in what is called specialty care. This is for Dementia patients, which are usually afflicted with Alzheimer's disease. Many assisted living facilities have developed part of their area just for the care of Dementia patients. Also some of these facilities have completely converted to specialty care. Nursing homes usually combine this care with the main stream of patient care. Once you have to be in a nursing home, all forms of illnesses are taken care of together until death or recovery. I think nursing homes should separate the treatment of Dementia patients from other types of treatment. Treating Dementia patients with general maintenance care without any special attention to their needs can actually have a deleterious affect on them resulting in a shortened life.

How did my wife and I locate an assisted living facility for my mother? We did not know where any were located, what they provided or how much they cost. We had only been told generally about their level of care and that my mother would probably fit that level. This can be a scary situation when you have a deadline to work with. As I recall our starting point was the yellow pages. My first thought was to find a place that was not too far from home so as to facilitate visiting. I had visited Mother in the rehabilitation center every day due to her critical condition. We are thinking this new experience for her will take the same frequency of visits at least initially.

Well, my wife and I picked the first Assisted Living Community (ALC), out of the Yellow Pages that was closest to our home and called to set up an appointment. All of the looking we are doing is prior to my mother being released from the rehabilitation center. We arrived at the ALC and were happy to see it was a new looking building with nice landscaping. A very friendly person who said she was the assistant manager greeted us. She took us in to meet the manager. They were both friendly people and wanted to put us at ease right away. The manager wanted to know some pertinent information concerning Mother. The information was about her general health, how long she would be in the rehabilitation center and why did we think she was a candidate for an ALC. We described Mother's condition and she agreed based on our brief description that assisted living was a possibility. Also she was able to give us a close price for Mother's level of care. This price and her condition would be further evaluated after they visited Mother in the rehabilitation center and also, after she had been under care for 30 days. Usually the price remains the same. The manager invited us to look at the various types of apartments that were available. The apartments were new and were available in studio, one-bedroom and two-bedroom styles. Most ALC's have the latest senior amenities built in to the apartments. Fairly standard items would be walk-in shower stalls with no step, shower spray attachment, folding shower seat, colored toilet seat for depth perception and toilet hand bars. Some of these places allow you to put in your own specialty items.

There are a few thoughts to consider when choosing an apartment. We wanted Mother to be in comfortable familiar surroundings, but be able to get around her place without much effort. She had been used to a one-bedroom apartment before her fall. We didn't want her to have to take a step down in living style so we had our minds geared to that end. I do think you have to put this thinking aside sometimes, depending on how mobile your family member is. The more room to walk the more chance there is to fall. We felt my mother was steady enough with her walker and the assistance she would have, that a one-bedroom would be fine. There is validity to the idea that a studio apartment in some cases provides more safety as long as it is not cluttered.

We discussed the care Mother would receive from the nurses and CNA's. This might be a good time to take a general look at this subject. There are various levels of care provided by an ALC besides the specialty care I mentioned previously. Not all ALC's have the special Dementia care. Certain restructuring and new rules set by the government have to be adopted by the facility. The regular assisted living levels of care are based on the amount of attention and services the ALC provides. The basic level 1 means that a resident can do everything for themselves, but needs occasional minor assistance with bathroom, grooming and dressing activities. What will be added to a level 1 is a medication management fee. ALC residents are not allowed to administer their own medicine. The levels go up about seven price points beyond the basic level. The various levels above level 1 can be specifically defined or just level numbers with prices. It's best to get these levels specifically defined rather than deal with them subjectively. I wanted something in writing for my mother's level so I could have something to compare against her actual care. I believe this clarification is essential to avoid floating price levels. They do re-evaluate in a month or so, depending on the ALC, so it's best not to start with unnecessary care and services. The services are what can be inflated the easiest. Laundry, telephone services, expanded housekeeping are things you may not want to sign for initially. Of course the care my mother was to receive was the most important consideration. The greatest portion of the care is centered on the CNA's. The patient to CNA ratio is very important to know. This is an industry that is notoriously understaffed therefore this information should be carefully evaluated. The range for this data is generally six to nine residents per CNA. The preferred would be closest to the six to one ratio, but it is not normal to find this. A manager may tell you that they have a desirable patient to CNA ratio but it is hard to verify this unless you have the total resident count and the total number of CNA's on staff. Then you have some variables such as how many are very part time and what is the average absentee rate per week. Believe it or not demographics can play a big part in the quality of care. Basically for a level 1 resident the attention from a CNA is hourly. From the outset, to do a rough check on this, you need to visit for a few hours every day. After Mother was located in an ALC, I found that there were individual resident logbooks updated daily by the CNA's. They are available for family review. The information in the logbooks is useful for all of the staff, including the nursing staff. The logbook enables everyone to obtain information and to log in medical changes and needs that may occur in a resident. Some pertinent information comes from the family through the initial entrance process. This can be information such as resident likes and dislikes, critical medical information, and sleeping or eating habits. Information is logged as to how often a resident is attended to by a CNA. Later after Mother was in an ALC I did personally observe a couple of CNA's sitting in a corner late in the day filling out their day's information in just a few minutes. This could make one doubtful of timely resident attention. All ALC's have a nursing staff on site. Generally these are Registered Nurses (RN's) and Licensed Practical Nurses (LPN's). When an RN is on duty it is usually during the day shift. This is because an RN due to their advanced skill level, versus an LPN's skill level can only perform certain duties. More attention of this type is warranted during the day shift. Sometimes an RN works part time and is on call the balance of the time. At least one LPN is on duty every day shift and only sometimes at night. The manager of this first place told us they did not employ an RN and that the LPN was part time. We really didn't see a CNA staff roaming around. The manager said at this time they only had three or four CNA's, but sometimes she and the assistant manager would fill in. Their total number of residents was about forty-five. My wife and I were not too excited about this place mainly due to our perception that her care could be lacking. In a few days we brought Mother to visit this first ALC. We weren't sure how she would react to living in this environment or if she remembered discussing it. Mother went through the motions and was very cooperative, but at the end of the tour she told us she didn't care for the manager or the people that lived there. I guess this was predictable.

Generally the food at ALC's is not too bad. Food taste can vary from place to place. Some places tout their chefs as coming from previously auspicious venues. From sampling food at various locations, I believe the preparation of different recipes does make a difference however small. Most places use similar or the same food distributors which keeps the quality fairly even. You will be paying a bit extra for presentation and recipe flair. The ALC's I encountered all provided three meals per day plus snacks. The main hot meal can either be at noon or at five or six in the evening. Snacks are generally in the afternoon and consist of cookies, ice cream, fruit or candy. Basically if a resident is hungry, they can have just about anything at any time.

The handling of medications is standard at the places I encountered. The ALC buys all the medications based on the resident's prescriptions.

By law the purchase has to be made from a pharmacy that prepares the medicine in bubble packs. The ALC has a place of this type that they deal with. You are locked in to using their pharmacy. Yes, the medicine is much more expensive than what you could buy yourself some where else. Sometimes you can work in some antibiotic cream or antacid on your own, but it has to be kept out of view because of regulations.

They are very strict concerning medicine distribution. LPN's and RN's are the only staff allowed to administer medications. A person on limited medication can have a monthly charge of one or two hundred dollars for the medicine, but these charges can be sometimes filed with your supplemental insurance carrier.

Every ALC has an activity director to coordinate various group activities and functions. It is this person's job to help everyone enter into activities that promote physical and mental stability. Usually you can meet the activities director at preliminary meetings. This person should have some credentials and tenure in this field. A factor in their success is if they are dedicated and tolerant. There are functions that families can take part in and there are also outside excursions for residents if they desire. My mother unfortunately did not want to participate in any activities.

Security consists of locking doors after five or six p.m. and having a desk attendant on duty with a sign in sheet. The night attendant does make rounds to check everything. If the ALC is totally dedicated to Dementia patients, then there is a twenty four-hour lock down. This means no one, including family can get into the building at any time without being let in by a staff member. All residents of a Dementia unit are also under lock down, although they can have their own apartment key.

My wife and I looked at about six ALC's prior to Mother's release from rehabilitation. We took her to visit the ones that we thought were best. We went to the complimentary lunches that most offer. We talked to everyone on the front lines, managers, directors, nurses and some general staff when available. We toured the apartments and the grounds. It is really a task to find a place of this type that is best in every way for your family member, especially when you do not have any experience. Since only pre-purchased long-term care insurance pays for assisted living needs, you need to find a place that has the best care for the best value. The base price ranges we found in our area for a one-bedroom apartment were from eighteen hundred dollars to thirty-five hundred dollars per month. This is quite a chunk of money to pay out of one's savings, but in my mother's situation there was no choice. The insurance my mother had was Medicare and supplemental Blue Cross/Blue Shield, which only pays Major Medical, doctors' visits, medicines, tests and therapy. I say "only", but this is great coverage especially if you are sick along the way. Institutional costs are still a huge financial drain on personal finances.

We investigated ALC's as much as possible for the time constraint we had. It was time to pick a place for Mother to live. We chose a one bedroom assisted living apartment that was fifteen minutes from our home.

CHAPTER SIX

LIVING WITH ASSISTANCE

As we left Mother in chapter four, she was leaving the rehabilitation center walking with her walker with my wife and me close by. A local mover had moved all of Mother's furniture from her old apartment. We wanted all of her furniture in place for her arrival so the apartment would look and feel homey upon arrival. After going to lunch we headed for her assisted living home. I'm not sure after talking at lunch that Mother knew if she was going to her old apartment or to someplace new. Recently we had been briefing her about living where she would have some help doing things. She seemed okay with it at the time but I'm not sure how long she retained that information.

We arrived at the ALC and met with Elizabeth, the Director of Assisted Living, to fill out the entrance paperwork. The paperwork consists of getting Mother's and my signature agreeing to their policies and terms. There are no leases due to the age and circumstances of the resident. The only commitment I had was to make payments in case of any monetary exhaustion on Mother's part. There was a seven hundred-dollar entrance fee that would be applied to the rent after six months. The base rent for this place was eighteen hundred and ninety-five dollars per month. We finished the checking-in procedures and were ready to take Mother to her apartment on the third floor. I was not sure what was going to happen when Mother entered the apartment. My wife and I, Elizabeth and Mother arrived at the door to see a nice wreath attached to her nameplate. Elizabeth said this was a complimentary wreath that all new residents receive. I unlocked the door and in we went. At first Mother was surprised and didn't say much. As we explained how her apartment was setup and that it was all her personal belongings, she was very happy to the point of crying. It actually looked better than her old place because we had dressed up the new place a little more. She was more than happy as she walked around. As I said before, of the ones we looked at, this apartment was the best value. The rooms were spacious with good closet space. This complex had been converted from a regular apartment house to assisted living. The bathroom lacked having senior friendly items except for toilet hand bars and a spray shower attachment. The kitchen had a full size refrigerator and roomy cabinets. The only thing we had to do was finish hanging a few pictures. The location of the apartment was very convenient for meals. All Mother had to do was walk across the hall into the dining room. A dining room CNA would come over to remind Mother about meals and walk over with her. There was a dining room on each floor with a kitchen attached. Meals were brought around to each person at a table. The food was hot mainly because the dining area was small enough that nothing had a chance to get cold when served. CNA's are on duty to help with any utensil skills that may be lacking. Menus are published for the week so everyone can get a chance to see what meals are coming. There is an alternate main dish and more than one or two side dishes. This allows the resident a choice and it can be made at the time the meals are served. Sometimes the kitchen can get you something else other than the choices on your floor's menu. Each floor has a different menu so different foods can be obtained. Residents can come to this dining room for juice, milk and various snacks at any time or wait for the afternoon snack. Each resident would sit at the same table for every meal. New residents, like my mother, would start at a new table with one or two people. My wife and I stayed with Mother for supper to help her along in the new surroundings. We all sat at a table near the kitchen with two other ladies, one being new. The CNA asked Mother if the current menu was okay and she said that it was. Food was served and we all had a good meal. After supper we took Mother back to her apartment to talk and watch television. There were two CNA's and an LPN on Mother's floor that we were getting to know quickly. They were very nice and my mother seemed to like them fairly well. The CNA's were to come in and check on Mother every hour or less since she was just getting acclimated. We were apprehensive about leaving for the evening, but we had talked to everyone concerned and felt comfortable. Mother would be helped at bedtime, asked if she needed to go to the bathroom and given any medicine that was on her chart. As I recall the only medicines that followed her from rehabilitation in bubble pack were aspirin and the appetite enhancer.

The next day my wife and I went to visit Mother shortly before lunch. Her apartment door was ajar so we knocked and went in to find her in the bedroom going through her dresser drawers. She had her walker in front of her as she stood in front of the dresser. She decided that this was a good time to visit with us and watch a little television.

I wanted to find someone who could tell me how her first night went. A CNA on day shift said she had heard Mother didn't want to go to bed until late and that she wanted to sleep in later the next morning, which were her sleeping habits most of her later life. Meanwhile the morning shift gets her up at six-thirty for breakfast. The house rule is all residents have to be fully dressed if going to the dining room. I was aware of the early rise and also knew Mother did not like to get up that early. We asked Elizabeth, the director, if Mother could get up later and just have coffee, juice and toast in her room. She said she would pass the word down to the charge nurse. In talking with Mother in her apartment, she was wondering how long she would be there and when she was going home. This was discouraging because we thought she would come around when she saw her own belongings. We told her that this was home and everything was hers and she would get used to everything. Mother was very aware of what was going on but still had the short-term memory problem.

Everything was going well the first week. The staff and Mother were coping well with each other except for the late nights and early mornings. I guess Mother was cranky and a little trouble to get going that early. We were still working on having her get up a little later.

Unfortunately, to say the least, I received a call from the ALC that was not pleasant, especially after all that everyone had been through. Mother had fallen in her apartment and had pain in her left shoulder. I told the nurse to have the local ambulance service, HEMSI, take her to the hospital and we would meet her there. As we arrived they were taking her to x-ray. Mother said she was in pain but otherwise she was chipper. We noticed she was in her slippers and not regular shoes. We had told the staff at her place not to let Mother wear slippers during the day, because she didn't have any support, and therefore she had less balance. We believe these slippers contributed to her fall, but I could do nothing about it. It took the usual amount of time for evaluation until the verdict was in. Mother had a crack in the bone just below the shoulder socket. This would not require hospital stay but would require being in a sling for seven weeks. Nothing else was to be done for the healing process. Mother was taken back to her apartment in the early evening of the same day. This was about six p.m. and mother had missed her supper. The staff brought supper to her apartment so she could eat at her own dining table. The CNA'S and nurses were coming to Mother's room to discuss how they would care for her with the new injury. The staff was saying Mother needed too much specialized treatment and they were not equipped to handle her in assisted living. Their main problem was having to devote two people to mother for bathroom, dressing and dining duties on a more frequent basis. My argument was this was assisted living and I didn't see why two people had to attend mother all the time. I was losing the battle. The charge nurse called Elizabeth, the director, and told me Elizabeth had a suggestion. Her plan was to have a sitter for a day or two and see how it works out. Elizabeth relayed the telephone number of a reliable sitter service that had worked at this ALC. The sitter idea was completely foreign to us, as is most everything new that happens. The sitter is a person that sits with someone that needs constant attention. This is done on a shift basis or a twenty-four hour basis. The cost for this service ranges from seven dollars an hour to thirteen dollars an hour. Yes, the resident pays for this. This service is considered a luxury and not reimbursed by insurance. We were in a tight spot, so I called the sitter service to get someone for the rest of the evening and for a few days until this situation was settled. These services are on call at a moment's notice and there are no contracts to sign. At approximately eight p.m. a lady in her late fifties came to the door. She introduced herself as Dora from the sitter service. We sat and talked for a while going over her experience. She had been a CNA for years at various types of institutions that dealt with the elderly. This means she was experienced at helping with a person's daily living activities. I gave her Mother's history and told her about her current condition and that I wanted her watched very closely. Dora was going to work until seven a.m. when another person would come for the twelve-hour day shift. I asked Dora to fill in the new person as to Mother's condition. We had a talk with Mother's regular staff as to how they will interface with the sitters. They said they would still do their duties, but use the sitter's assistance. I did learn that typically sitters would not do more than assist a resident in doing daily living activities although, it depends on the nature of your sitter. Regardless, it seemed as though there was an overlap of services and payment in this situation. We had to bear with it for now even if it was for some added safety for my mother in her present condition. Later I will go into some of the pros and cons of having sitters.

I called Elizabeth Monday morning to see what her recommendations were. She said they couldn't give mother the proper care in assisted living due to the cracked shoulder. The alternatives would be to use around-the-clock sitters where she is now, or move her downstairs to the nursing home section. To stay where she is, with the sitters, would be more expensive and the nursing care would be less than she needs. In the assisted section the cost is about two thousand dollars per month for their service, plus four thousand dollars per month for the sitting service. The nursing section costs about half of all that. I hated to put Mother in a nursing home knowing how they are. I did try to argue that Mother would be better off in her own surroundings, but I knew the care would be lacking. So, we had to tell Mother that she would be going downstairs for a seven-week convalescence. By the way, one reason we selected this complex was that it has independent living, assisted living and nursing care under one umbrella. We thought this transition would be easier if something happened rather than going through everything it would take to make a transfer somewhere else. Also her assisted apartment rent would be suspended while she is getting well, and the apartment is kept for her. They do this if the resident is expected to return. I'm not so sure this is done if that apartment is the only one left to rent. Usually these places have a few vacancies most of the time.

CHAPTER SEVEN

A BRIEF NURSING HOME STAY

We moved Mother downstairs to the nursing unit. Her room was a semi-private, which again she was not happy with, not being a social person. Unfortunately Mother had to start using a wheelchair because of her arm being in a sling. Our fear about this was her legs becoming weak from lack of use. The nursing unit has its own therapy unit. They said they would apply to Medicare for payment approval for any therapy work. They didn't think there would be a problem even though Mother had therapy a short time ago. There is a time period restriction between therapy sessions, but this time the cause was not the same. Medicare did authorize payment for a certain amount of sessions with an evaluation after that.

We were totally naive concerning nursing home operations. You hear a lot about nursing homes with most of it not being good. Due to Mother's condition and age, I thought I should make daily visits to see how the care and treatment was. When I visited each day, mostly with my wife, Mother knew why she was there, and she didn't like it. I would still get the "When am I going home?" statement.

Staffing was set up the same as I described earlier. There are more RN's and LPN's on duty, but the resident to CNA ratio is probably on the deficient end due to increased resident need. Of course the staff's daily sick calls do nothing to help the situation.

The food program was set up with the usual three meals per day plus snacks. The kitchen was down the hall so the meals were brought over on carts. The plates of food were covered to maintain the heat. The residents would gather in the two dining rooms very early prior to each meal. Some of the residents, like Mother, had to be brought to the table by the CNA. The CNA's had their own roster of residents that they were responsible for. I was coming in every day for either lunch or supper to see how Mother was eating. A lot of times I would be early and took her to the dining room when it was time. This entailed pushing the wheelchair from her room to the dining room and positioning her at the correct table. Sometimes I would stay and prep her food with seasonings or cut certain food items. These were things hard for Mother to do with one arm. The sling arm was slightly usable for light work if Mother just used her fingers. A lot of the time I stayed back and didn't acknowledge I was there. I wanted to see if Mother was brought to her meals on time and how much the CNA's helped her deal with getting started to eat. They seemed to do pretty well helping the people that needed help. On one occasion I arrived late for lunch and didn't see Mother at her table nor was she in her room. I went looking in the hallways until I found her pedaling her wheelchair at the far end of the dining room hall. She appeared to be looking for her room. I went to the nurse's station and showed the charge nurse what was going on. She had Mother's CNA get her and bring her to lunch. They said they would have gotten her, but lunch was already half over. When Mother saw me she said, "Where have you been"? She was starting to forget I was visiting everyday.

The nursing home section had a doctor and one of the RN's make rounds to every resident on Thursday mornings. Family was allowed to participate much the same as in the rehabilitation center. If you arrived early enough and the doctor knew you were there, he would go right to you as soon as possible. My wife and I would partake to tell the doctor how we thought Mother was doing, along with her view, and discuss her medicines. Mother was physically doing fairly well in the beginning. A consistent problem she had was not going to the bathroom enough coupled with not drinking ample fluids. We talked to the doctor about possibly discontinuing Detrol, a bladder control drug, which can promote dryness. She had only been taking this medicine for a short time. Obviously we could not keep track of Mother's bathroom habits so I spoke to the Director of Nursing. She said they had a B and B sheet, bowel and bladder, that is put on the bathroom door for the CNA's to do daily bathroom tracking and commenting. They put this into action right away. Mother had been in the nursing home section for about two weeks. Her weight was going down and she was feeling depressed. There was really no progress to notice concerning her shoulder. It was to heal just by being in a sling and not using it. X- rays were scheduled in about two weeks to look at the healing process. Her short-term memory was not any better. Mother was not remembering any of my visits. She seemed depressed not being able to walk and especially having one arm tied down. Therapy was going to start three times per week to work on her legs. It was to be very mild exercises to keep strength and muscle tone alive. The first feedback I received about Mother going to therapy was that she was very stubborn about going. She went down to the therapy center but would not let anyone do anything for her. My first thought was that she was too afraid of falling again. I told them I would accompany her the next time she had an appointment.

It was a day or two from Mother's ninety-second birthday. My brother and his wife were coming to town to help celebrate. Mother was not feeling very well and looked gaunt and in distress. She wasn't eating or drinking enough to keep her going. Stomach pains had started to bother her fairly often. When my brother arrived he noticed how bad she looked. We wanted to go on with the birthday party and try to cheer her up. I reserved a party room that the nursing home has available for special occasions. The room is free, with nice furnishings, and the food is from their food service, which is served by the kitchen staff. There is a small meal charge for guests other than the resident. I bought a birthday cake and some balloons to make a party atmosphere. Everything was ready as we brought Mother down to the party room in her wheelchair. She did not look or feel well. In fact this was the worst I had seen her look since the first fall. Her face was very sunken and had a painful expression. One of Mother's favorite CNA's from assisted living came to the party to cheer her up and have cake. We opened the presents we had gotten her and tried to help her get through the party. She was in pain and had to go to the bathroom so the CNA took care of her. When she came back, there didn't seem to be much relief. We decided Mother had enough for the day so we took her back to her apartment to rest. I still had keys for the apartment in assisted living and we would take her back for a visit now and then to keep up her morale. That day ended with my brother getting ready to leave the next day. I don't think he ever expected to see her alive again. I remember telling him at the airport that we would bring her back to better health.

Mother was still having a battle with stomach pains. The nurses were giving her a pain reliever that was making her very sleepy. I inquired about this and they said it was a narcotic base. At this time I was visiting twice a day because she didn't seem well. Also because of her poor appetite, the appetite enhancer was started again. This is something we had previously decided on at a recent doctor's meeting prior to any stomach problem. Her weight was down to ninety-seven pounds. People of Mother's size, five-foot and small boned, that are less than one hundred pounds should be watched carefully.

For the next few days we watched her closely. The stomach was a problem most of the time. Her eating was off and on. I would bring Mother a sundae when I would come back in the evening. Although Mother was only taking the painkiller on an as needed basis, she was lethargic most of the time. We saw the doctor at the next scheduled meeting and relayed her problems. He thought a lot of her problems were bowel related and wanted to give her a laxative. I had noticed at lunch the other day that she was being given a very thick yellowish drink. The doctor said it was a high calorie drink he wanted to continue. He also wanted to start a medicine for depression. It seemed like a lot of medicine for a little frail person, but he's the doctor.

We took Mother to her scheduled appointment with the doctor who was taking care of her shoulder. The X-rays showed normal healing which was very promising for someone Mother's age. The doctor said Mother could unstrap her sling at mealtime. There was still to be no pressure put on the shoulder, which meant no walking with her walker.

Mother was still lethargic and not eating or drinking well enough. The Director of Nursing, Jan, thought she might do better in the other dining area where residents that can't or won't eat, are helped and prodded more. I was not for this because I thought that being in that room would take away what dexterity skills she had left, plus most of the people there were very below her health level. Well, I agreed to give it a trial run if it meant Mother possibly eating and drinking more. I was still coming in everyday especially now due to the new eating arrangement. The first day of the dining room change, I found Mother in the old location. I checked and the staff had not been notified of the change. I thought since I had agreed to this arrangement I had better follow through and see someone about the change. It took a few meals for the staff to get in sync. I let the CNA's do there job and help the eating process along. My Mother didn't seem to do any better getting the extra prodding;

also some of the people sitting close to Mother bothered her due to their actions. The people can't help it but my mother of course couldn't understand this. No one at these tables uttered a word of conversation; therefore there was not any stimulation of this nature. After a few days of this I told Jan to put Mother back in her old mode of eating. This brought on a couple more instances of Mother wandering off down the hall at mealtime. With the dining room change again, the staff was unsure as to her location the first couple of days. This was the old communication problem raising its head again.

Mother was still mostly in discomfort and pain. Over the last week the doctor, nursing staff and I had been trying everything we knew to bring her around. She was taking medicine for appetite, pain, depression and a mild laxative. Also she was on the high calorie drink at suppertime. This one I had stopped a few days ago because Mother would not drink it. I tasted it and it was a very foul tasting liquid. Mother would have occasional good reports on her eating. After each meal a CNA would go around and assign an arbitrary percentage to the amount of food eaten. This was recorded in her chart and was available to me.

I arrived at a ten a.m. appointment one day to talk to a Psychologist that the staff said they occasionally set up with families to help them cope.

I talked to him for a half-hour and had a pleasant conversation. He really wasn't specifically knowledgeable of Mother's case, so I didn't get a lot of useful data. After our meeting I went to visit my mother and found her in the hall in her wheelchair in terrible pain. She was also spitting up a greenish liquid. I had the charge nurse get someone to put her to bed right away. They gave her milk of magnesia to ease the pain. At this point I had enough and ran over to the Director of Nursing's office and said, "Give my mother an enema immediately or send her to the hospital." She ran to get the charge nurse and an LPN to start the ball rolling. I told Mother she was going to have an enema and she wasn't too happy. It didn't matter too much to me at that time because I just wanted some action. The staff doesn't really want to send a resident to a hospital for something they should be able to handle. Well, the enema was administered and the amazing happened; no stomach pains. Mother was feeling much better and wanted to take a nap. I returned for supper and found Mother sitting at her table waiting to eat. She said she did not have any stomach pains and was feeling pretty well. Over the next couple of days I visited twice a day. We felt this was a critical time for Mother. She had to start feeling better and eating better. Her weight could not go down anymore and she needed to walk. I went to therapy with Mother to help them with her disposition. She was cranky about going and refused to do her leg exercises. My wife and I were able to convince her to do a few. It was an uphill battle, but therapy said that they would keep trying especially to walk her in the hallways using her walker. We were going to push Mother to her goal of being well enough to go back to her ALC apartment. She was improving at a good rate after her stomach battle. We cut her medicine down to a calcium pill, a vitamin pill, the appetite enhancer (pill form), and a daily laxative pill.

I was kidding the Director of Nursing about this new marvel of medicine called an "enema". She laughed, but said, "We really don't have a strong bowel management program here". I didn't comment too much although I thought if this place, which was pretty good, doesn't have a program, what about other nursing homes? I really believe that simple problems left to neglect can develop into deathly situations.

We picked Mother up one afternoon to take her to our house for supper. We weren't sure how well she would hold up since this was her first outing of this type. Mother got so tired that she put her head down on the dining room table and fell asleep. We took her back to the nursing home in time to catch her evening meal. Mother was also starting to complain about burning at urination. I asked the charge nurse to put her back on the medicine for the urinary tract infection, (UTI). We went through the same treatment procedures for identifying the strain of infection as we did in the rehabilitation center. Mother's spirits and appetite were still improving. She was at times eating well over fifty percent of her meals. The appetite enhancer was certainly being very effective.

On my next visit Mother was in the hall in her wheelchair. Her arm strap was off and the charge nurse said that the visiting doctor told her that she could take it off. Not being tied down did help her eat a little better. I made sure everyone knew she could not bear weight on her shoulder.

I wanted Mother to try and stand, leaning against her bed for support. I helped her out of her wheelchair and walked her to her bed. I watched her as she stood and moved from one end of her bed to the other straightening her bed sheets. This was encouraging even though we had been helping her walk in the hall with her holding on to the railing with one hand, and my wife and I balancing her.

I wanted to help Mother's mind stay as alert as possible. We would go to the recreation area and play poker. We would stick with one type of game so it was familiar each time. She really had no problem playing the game. Other times I would let her play solitaire, which does require some thinking and she was actually better at this. Our only goal was to have Mother back in her assisted living apartment. Occasionally we would take Mother to her apartment after supper for ice cream, which was easy for her because it was only an elevator's ride away.

One morning about eleven fifteen I went into Mother's room and found her still in bed with no clothes on and no bed sheets, only a thin cover to pull over her. I asked her what was going on but she didn't know. I ran to the nurse's station to get the charge nurse and take her back down to Mother's room. Obviously I was in a bad way with the situation and told them what I thought. I got every excuse you could think to say. The main excuse was four CNA's called off for the day shift and no one knew who was to take care of Mother. Evidently someone had started Mother's day, quit and no one else came on. These are not unusual circumstances. I guess it's possible that she could have missed lunch and been in bed for hours had I not come in to visit.

Mother was due for her doctor's appointment to look at her shoulder. We were hoping she would be able to put weight on it to enable her to use her walker. The verdict was that it is strong enough because of the healing process and some cartilage had also grown around that area. This was good news that her recuperation was on schedule. After her appointment we went to out to supper and back to her room. If it's food she likes, Mother will eat at least eighty-percent. We were having Mother use her walker as much as possible when she would go to her apartment. We would supervise her walking up and down the hall in front of her place. This could be as much as forty feet at one time. She wasn't too happy about it, but we persevered anyway. Lately Mother had been walking to most of the meals that I have gone to and sat in a normal chair. Since Mother was not a "regular" walker, meaning she was using a wheelchair most of time, no one walked her to other meals. Therapy was having a little better time with Mother, walking her three times a week. The reports on her were that she was very steady using her walker.

Mother was looking and eating very well. Her weight was only ninety-eight pounds, but it had been stable. Mother was also getting up out of a chair and going to the bathroom by herself. All this we considered to be a minor miracle due to her being in such bad shape on her birthday four weeks prior. We had Mother's hair fixed at the beauty shop in the nursing home. They would come to get her and take her back to her room after giving her a haircut or whatever she was having done that day.

Mother's two granddaughters were coming to visit on this particular weekend. They had heard how down she was a short while ago and wanted to see her. Both girls are around thirty years old and married. Shari lives in Virginia and Heather in Michigan. We picked them up at the airport and went right to Mother's place. They were astonished at how well she looked. She was dressed in a nice suit, hair fixed and using the walker alone. The girls spent all the time with Mother that was possible, which was only the two days they were here. We all were together in her apartment talking and looking at old pictures trying to get Mother back in touch as much as possible. We would bring food in for meals or get it from the dining area across the hall. Everyone had a good time eating and socializing, especially Mother. This was probably some of her best medicine. Well, time flew by and the girls had to return home.

A few days before the girls arrived, I went to see the Assistant Director of Operations, Sue, and I told her that I felt that Mother could go back to her assisted living apartment next week. We discussed her progress and I filled her in on where I believed her level to currently be. She was attentive and very nice, but I could see she was not the decision-maker. Sue said that she would have to get certain people to concur with my recommendation before we could go forward. This meant the nurses, the house doctor, the Director of Nursing, the Director of Operations and the Director of Assisted Living. I knew this was quite a list to satisfy, but I thought Mother was up to the task. A couple of days went by and I received a call from Elizabeth, the Director of Assisted Living. She said that Mother could go back to her apartment in a couple of days depending on the paperwork being completed in that time frame. The next day I contacted the charge nurse, Carla, who was responsible for getting the go ahead from the house doctor. She had faxed the paperwork to him but did not receive any reply as yet. Mother was still feeling fine and eating as well as expected. I told Mother what was going on and she seemed happy to be going back to her place. Although to my surprise there was some apathy about the move. She seemed a little afraid to leave her current situation. I think it was because of the help and care she believed she was getting and that going back to her apartment would be giving up her security. I told her she would have assistance and a lot more privacy in her old apartment. As far as care goes, it is a hard comparison between assisted living and a nursing facility. It really depends on your level of health. If your health is stable and you are on maintenance or short-term recovery, the attention you receive in the nursing area is probably less. Except for meals and medicine, you are left alone for hours at a time in the nursing home, versus hourly checks in assisted living. This is saying that ALC's follow through with the hourly checks that most propose.

I received a call that I was not expecting or wanting from Carla the charge nurse, who was taking care of the final paperwork from the house doctor. She said the doctor would let mother go to her own apartment if she had twenty-four hour sitters with her. This was a real shock, after everyone involved had told me it was a done deal. I wonder now if people knew what was coming and let the doctor do the dirty work. The next morning happened to be the time of the doctor's next rounds. I expressed my concerns about this to him, especially the monetary aspect. He said he was looking out for Mother's best interest but wanted to see for himself how she was progressing. Mother was sitting in a regular chair in her room, so the doctor asked her to get up by herself and use her walker to go over to the bathroom. Mother made a huge effort to do this and looked good doing it. The doctor asked mother to go to the toilet and sit down just to see if she could. She sat down and then raised up on her walker and went back to her chair. The doctor was surprised and said, " You are better than I thought you were." IIe thought we might step up the walking therapy and he would consider this again in two weeks. We got together with the main people involved to formulate a rejuvenated walking program. Mothers' Day arrived so my wife and I took Mother out to one of her favorite places for brunch. She was looking very well and using her walker totally alone with my wife or me close by for quick support. She did a great job of eating, probably ninety-percent, and seemed in good spirits. After brunch we spent time in her apartment having some ice cream and watching television. She seemed much the same as when she first left the rehabilitation center.

In the summer my wife and I go to a couple of tennis tournaments. We were wondering how to tell Mother about the trip or would she understand and remember where we were. She gets worried when I'm not around but her memory is not that good to always know what is going on. We decided to tell Mother we were making this trip. It was only for four days, which shouldn't put much stress on her. While we were away we called Mother a couple of times to give her peace of mind. She did remember we were away and said she was having fun with the dogs that the nursing home often provides as therapy. Mother loves animals especially dogs. This is really some of the best therapy there is for cheering up older people, providing they care for dogs.

We went to see Mother the day after we arrived home. We did find some disturbing things that had been happening. Mother's dentures were not in her mouth and her hearing aid was under the bed. She can't communicate intelligently without the aid. Her eyeglasses were at the bottom of the clothes hamper in a sweater pocket. When we are there, we take care of all of this on a daily basis. One of the CNA's told us Mother's hearing aid was not in her ear for two days. One would think that the CNA who prepared her for the day would recognize and make an effort to correct the situation. We were able to get Mother to walk down the hall. The therapist said she showed some improvement working with our plan to review Mother in two weeks. She had Mother in her apartment trying to familiarize her with the surroundings so moving back would not be such a shock. My wife and I watched her walk up and down the hallway, which seemed to verify therapy's assessment. Another walk we took was outside to Mother's car so she could see something else familiar. She always liked to wash and take care of her cars. Generally speaking Mother was doing very well in her mobility and her grooming. She was undressing herself at night and getting into bed by herself. She stands at the bathroom mirror and puts on her make-up and also goes to the bathroom alone. At this point Mother was in good spirits and seemed to be progressing towards moving back upstairs. One thing bothering me was a couple of charge nurses telling me that Mother was saying strange things and occasionally having delusions.

I went to see the Director of Nursing to find out if she had heard anything new in relation to Mother moving to her apartment and to discuss her current condition. She said that Elizabeth, the Director of Assisted Living did not want Mother back. She thought it was because of under staffing and insurance reasons. I went to see Elizabeth to find out what was going on with this whole situation. I confronted her with what I was told and she said that she really didn't have anything against Mother moving back and that it was actually up to the health care group. I was in a dilemma so I had the Director of Nursing set up a meeting with the interested parties for the next Tuesday.

Things were still going smoothly with Mother, but I had not heard any word on the meeting. I went to the Director of Nursing's office to see what the delay was and she told me she was under the impression Elizabeth was to call and make the arrangements. She also said the consensus of opinion was that they weren't going to let Mother go back to her apartment. Obviously this news was very discouraging along with the feeling that something else was happening. The confusion of contradiction and miscommunication made us wonder if a decision had been made and they didn't really want to tell us until they let us exhaust every last option.

The meeting did finally take place. My wife and I met with the various directors we had talked to previously including a new person, the house Social Director. I knew I had to make a strong case for Mother because we felt the deck was stacked against her. I took some of what you might call before and after pictures to the meeting. These pictures were of Mother at her worst and of her at her recovery peak while in the nursing center. I used these along with a variety of milestones we thought mother had achieved. Everyone listened intently and politely without much opposition. After I was through, Jan, the Director of Nursing started with her views on Mother's progress. She started by talking about some incidents that had happened recently. She said that Mother had been sitting outside on the porch, which she hates to do, and when asked to come inside, Mother started toward the parking lot gate in her wheelchair. I had heard this a few days ago but passed it off as not being true. I couldn't believe Mother would do this, not being too brave when it came to being alone outside. Jan also said that Mother took the cord from her wheelchair alarm and threw it in the toilet, which caused it to clog. I guess I could believe this story because Mother was very stubborn at times. But, all this happened when I was out of town, which makes you wonder if they have an agenda. So, now their feeling is, with these incidents and a few other irrational comments Mother has made, they are concerned about her moving in a less than perfect mental state. I asked the group about the doctor's recommendation that Mother could move with twenty-four hour sitters. They were now worried about her mental state as much as her physical state. Reluctantly I proposed a month trial period with the sitters hoping that she would get even better in her own environment. They wanted to think this over and get back to me. The meeting adjourned on a cordial note.

Unfortunately we had to go out of town again and two days had passed since the meeting, with no word about the move. Elizabeth finally called and told me I could move mother on the twenty-first of June, after our trip. This was good news that Mother was getting out of the nursing home, but the thought of having sitters was not. We had already had a sitter for Mother the weekend she cracked her shoulder, so we knew where to start looking. I really wanted to know if there were any better companies that offered this service.

We thought Mother should have some companionship while we were away on our upcoming trip. This would also give me some experience with another sitter service. Some of the residents on Mother's nursing center floor have sitters, so I talked to one of them concerning a contact person. I made arrangements to meet this person at my mother's room to discuss having a sitter for Mother. We met one afternoon and I told him I wanted someone for a couple of hours each morning and each afternoon while we were away. I mentioned that Mother was going to have to have sitters for her trial month in her apartment. We discussed his hourly rate for the current job and he said that normally it is eleven dollars per hour, but for this short duration he would charge seven dollars per hour. I believe he was counting on our business in the future for Mother's trial period. He also knows that the service a lot of people use for seven dollars per hour is the one we previously used. I thought I would try this company instead of going back to the first one. I set everything up and told him we would meet the sitter on her first day just before we left for our trip. That day came and I was waiting at Mother's room at ten in the morning. A half-hour went by and no sitter. I walked past the room next to Mother's room and I saw a woman who looked like she was a sitter with a lady who had never had one. I casually asked her if she was a sitter and if she worked for the company that was supposed to provide someone for my mother next door. She had a strange look on her face and said that maybe she was to take care of Mother because this lady she was with now didn't think she was to have a sitter. I tried to keep from "losing it" because I was leaving very soon and didn't want to rock the boat. She came over to Mother's room after making a discrete exit from the other lady's room. Just then the fellow whom I had made the deal with came by and we straightened everything out. I have to admit I didn't leave with a very warm and fuzzy feeling. Mother was actually okay with the arrangement, realizing we were away and that somebody would be looking after her.

While we were away we checked in with the sitter by telephone. I told her I would do this at a set time allowing us to talk to her and mother. I called a day or two later and asked for the sitter. The staff had been aware of what I was doing and knew the sitter. But, unfortunately the sitter was not to be found anywhere, although it was her time to be with Mother. They said they would check to see when and if she had come to work. I knew right away I was at everyone's mercy and I may never know if the sitter was ever there. To my surprise, the next day I was able to talk with the sitter and Mother. She said she was a little late the other day, but stayed on to make up the time. At least Mother was fine, which was our main concern. The sitter said she had brought in some toy animals for Mother to have around her. This was a very good idea because Mother liked any kind of animal real or not. So, we felt good about this, knowing Mother was happy and that the sitter had thought to do this on her own and at her expense. I wanted a sitter for this trip for a couple of reasons. One being that it might help Mother get used to having someone like that around when she goes to her apartment. Another reason was to not have some of her things misplaced or not being used such as her hearing aid. I told the sitter before I left what had happened the last time we were away and for her to make sure it didn't happen this time. Her purpose was to fill in the times that Mother's CNA's left her unattended.

The trip was fine and Mother was able to come through our absence in good spirits. The long awaited move back to her ALC apartment was imminent. I was making some calls to sitter services to see if I could do any better for price or service. As I had mentioned earlier the pricing range in this area was from seven dollars per hour to thirteen dollars per hour. The service aspect is something you will not know about until you have the experience. I did experience some of the service for a day or two when Mother fell and cracked her shoulder. When talking to various services, they all seem to have the same inclusions and exclusions as far as what the sitter will do. Basically the sitter is there as a companion and to help the resident physically move about whether to move to the bathroom or meals. They generally won't clean up for any personal accidents, although it depends on the individual sitter. A sitter will make small snacks for the resident if the apartment has a kitchen or kitchenette. When a person needs a sitter, the safety net the sitter provides can be comforting for the family. A real challenge is to know when your family member needs a sitter especially in an ALC environment, and for what period of time. Would twenty four-hour services be necessary or would part-time services be adequate? If you utilize the services of a sitter, will the CNA's still perform the same duties they would ordinarily be responsible for without having a sitter? As far as the initial need for a sitter, I believe that is a situation that can only be resolved between a family and their physician. Don't let the monetary aspect be the number one deciding factor. The performance of the staff CNA's when a sitter is present is something that can be addressed and observed by the family. I'll go into some other pitfalls later using sitters and CNA's together. After limited checking, we chose the same sitter service we had before. It was the least inexpensive, seven dollars per hour, and none of the other services offered any thing significant to warrant a higher price. I believe other services had a much higher overhead rate than the one we selected. An older lady who had her business in her house ran the service we chose. This lady had provided this service to my mother's ALC for some time and had a good recommendation. This service was going to cost Mother about twelve hundred dollars per week or about five thousand per month, plus the approximately two thousand dollars per month for the apartment. So you see this is not a decision to be taken lightly. Remember, no insurance, unless you have long term care insurance (LTC), covers these costs. We figured we were in a corner and had to take this trial month with sitters or keep Mother in the nursing area with little hope of progression. Also

Stewart Nosky

I wanted to keep Mother out of a nursing home environment at any cost as long as there was hope of her doing better. I still believe that unless there is no possibility of recovery, a nursing home environment offers little chance of progression, if there is significant work to do and it is thought to be attainable. The whole premise of following this path for us was that we thought Mother would get to the point where she could get along with only the ALC CNA's. I guess I thought Mother was ready now, but the doctor and staff, as you know, thought otherwise. This compromise is probably best for Mother at least as far as her safety is concerned. The unknown is, will Mother do as we expect, and if not, what will the future bring? We are thinking she should improve based on her recent turn around and being in her own environment.

CHAPTER EIGHT

THE BIG DAY

Okay, the big day was here and up to the apartment we went. The sitter was scheduled to start on the evening shift at seven p.m. We had Mother walk up to her apartment so she would feel there was a real change coming. On her way up leaving the nursing area, she was waving and saying goodbye to every one she saw. I couldn't believe this was really happening after all we had gone through. She left her wheelchair behind; but in case she needed one, a brand new one was in her apartment that had been procured through Medicare when she left the rehabilitation center after first breaking her leg.

We arrived at Mother's apartment door to find a welcome back card in her mailbox from the staff. Mother unlocked her door and we all went in together. She looked around and seemed happy to be back. We showed Mother her apartment again to familiarize her with what she had as far as possessions and amenities. She had forgotten what had transpired recently and also wondered which things were hers and which were someone else's. I told Mother that everything in the apartment belonged to her and that this was her home.

It was getting near suppertime, so my wife and I decided to have supper with Mother in her dining room, which was out her door and four steps across the hall. If you can secure a room or apartment that is close to a nurse's station, or main nurse's room, or most importantly the dining room, it is a big plus for someone with impaired walking capabilities. We sat down with Mother at a table with three other ladies to wait for our food. The ladies were not too talkative and Mother is not that sociable at first, especially in a situation like this.

After supper we went to Mother's apartment to watch television and wait for the sitter who was to arrive at seven p.m. The sitter arrived on time and introduced herself as we showed her around. The staff CNA's came by to welcome Mother back to her apartment. The CNA's usually know the sitters from working together at Mother's ALC as well as from rotating work at other ALC's. This can be good and bad for a few reasons. If the CNA's know the sitter and like her, they could periodically check the resident while the sitter leaves her shift. This can obviously leave the resident in jeopardy without the required supervision Conversely, if they don't like each other, the CNA's could shirk their hourly checks, which could mean no help with bathroom functions. Remember most sitters do not offer much bathroom assistance beyond help to and from the bathroom. Also the sitter may end up having to be the one assisting the resident getting up and dressed in the morning, just when the sitters are changing shifts. I guess it's the luck of the draw if everyone gets along or not.

I wanted to go over a few things with Mother's sitter before we left for the evening. I showed her snacks that Mother had on hand in case she got hungry between meals, but I emphasized that Mother could get up on her own and make a peanut butter sandwich or get her own ice cream. Since this was a month's trial period, I felt I needed to know everything that was going on during the day and night from someone who was supposedly loyal to me. I gave her a sheet to fill out nightly and to pass on to the day shift with an explanation. The sheet had places to check yes or no concerning various CNA pertinent duties. It also had check places for Mother concerning bathroom and mealtime frequencies and percentages respectively. A big item on the sheet was how far Mother would walk each day with her walker while the sitter supervised. I wanted to know what Mother was doing day and night so I would have an unbiased opinion of her progress and also be able to help her with problems along the way. We wanted everything to go smoothly for Mother and to progress during the ensuing month to help insure her living without sitters in the future.

Our first meeting with the sitter was over and it was time the leave Mother for the evening. I don't think she totally realized the whole deal with the sitter, such as having someone around all the time, but she didn't seem afraid or upset. Our plan was to visit everyday for a while and then back off on our visits to let Mother get going more on her own.

The sitters were coming and going on their shifts and things seemed to be fairly smooth. I was relying on the status sheets I left with the sitters and talking to them in person to see how Mother was doing. Some of the things she was doing were not that conducive to progress. She was sleeping a lot of the day in her chair. The sitters were to walk her in the hallway at least a couple of times a day, but Mother was not too receptive to the idea. I believe she still saw the walker as an embarrassment, therefore she didn't want people to see her walking. The sleeping during the day kept mother awake too late in the evening. She did not want to go to bed until midnight, which did not fit with any plan the CNA's had for her. They wanted to have everyone in bed by eight-thirty so they could do other duties and not have to retrace their steps. Also bath times entered into the picture two to three times a week. Mother was not in favor of them giving her a bath, so that was a conflict. As long as Mother had a bath once a week, we thought bothering her about this more than that was too much for her. Due to Mother going to bed so late, which I had asked the staff to let her do, she did not want to get up at six-thirty in the morning. That led to reports of her being cranky and mean in the morning. If she went to bed early she was up through the night wanting something to eat or to go to the bathroom. We were able to work out a plan where Mother would get help with her bedclothes from a CNA about eight-thirty and be allowed to go to bed when she was tired. She then had to be allowed to get up a little later in the morning. This was acceptable, but tended to shift that burden to the sitter and that was really not her job. The CNA would not always come by Mother's apartment knowing she had someone there who would do the getting up tasks. If Mother missed the specific breakfast times, the sitter would make her coffee and toast right in Mother's own kitchen, which really was all she ate most of her life. This part was fine with the sitter and was under her area of duties. These events led to the CNA's drifting away from their responsibilities and Mother not trying to do some things she should be doing alone. When my wife and I would be with Mother we would have her get up out of her chair and walk her way over to her kitchen to make a peanut butter sandwich or get some ice cream from the refrigerator. I think the sitters found it easier to get these things for Mother themselves and also, Mother found it easier just to ask and have things handed to her. Mother used to make coffee by herself for years at least twice a day. Recently, she had not made coffee due to her meals being provided and the sitters making it for her. I thought it was time we got back into the groove of making coffee. I walked her over to the coffeepot and said, "Let's make some coffee today". She said, "Fine". So I got the coffee and filters down from the cabinet so we could start. I asked her to put the coffee into the filter, which I had already put in, and she scooped the coffee out of the can and stood motionless. She did not know where the filter apparatus was. I know this is hard to believe, but Mother did not remember any part of making coffee. I started to go step by step through the process and I could see how hard it would be to get this capability back.

This whole month's trial wasn't shaping up too well. Elizabeth had her staff keeping notes on Mother as I had the sitters do for me. Basically the staff's group was saying that Mother would be too hard to handle because of her sleep habits, being too confused to be alone and having some disagreements with the CNA's. At the time I was trying to suppress the bad stuff and magnify her good points to Elizabeth and her staff. In hindsight I think I agree with Elizabeth now, but at the time I thought that if they had the staff they were supposed to have and had the frequency of attendance they kept talking about, it could have worked out. I think deep down Elizabeth knew what her staff would and wouldn't do, so, I think that was the reality of the situation.

Time was ticking away and the end of the month was drawing near. I had some discussions with Elizabeth and she wasn't going to allow Mother to stay in her apartment without adequate supervision. Of course we could keep the sitters on at great expense and Mother could stay. Their only suggestion was to have her go back downstairs to the nursing home. There was no way we were going to let this happen.

This might be a good time to briefly discuss a couple of the pros and cons of having sitters. Sitters are expensive, but if you have the money, life with a sitter is much better from a comfort standpoint than being in a nursing home. If you have a dedicated sitter, she can often be a catalyst to help a person rehabilitate faster or at least stay even. This is probably not the normal occurrence. On the other hand, if you have a sitter for an extended period of time, she can do so much for the person she is sitting for, that the person loses the desire to do anything for him or herself. This can do the same as a nursing home does to shorten the person's life. Also, sitters sometimes may not be on duty when they are required to be. An example of this was a sitter of Mother's on the night shift had become tired and went to an empty room to sleep for a few hours. A friendly CNA on day shift told me she knew this to be true. Obviously this put Mother in danger during the night if she happened to get up to the bathroom, become hungry or had a heart attack or stroke. I related this to the sitter service and they said this sitter had done this before and they wouldn't send her out anymore. I think it depends on your financial position and the state of health of the person being cared for. It can be an alternative to going into a nursing home. My opinion is that nursing homes are where you go to die, and even in a shorter time than a few years ago. Over the last few years the average stay in a nursing home has decreased.

I was starting to prepare Mother for the move that was to be forthcoming. I wanted to make it sound as though she was going to move to a nicer place where she wouldn't have people breathing down her neck all the time. She had complained of having people around all the time. At the same time, I was honest with her about the whole situation because she was aware of the trial period. My wife and I had a meeting with the heads of the ALC to finalize what we already knew. Elizabeth had her stack of documents ready to answer any challenges I might have trying to persuade her to let Mother stay. I did not make one challenge because the die had been cast and I had other ideas for Mother. All I did was pick their brain as to what I should do with Mother, considering our resources and her condition. It boiled down to, in their opinion, that Mother should go back to their nursing area and maybe have a private room so she would be happier. I agreed to think about it and let them know. In the interim, they would see if a private room was available. In our minds the next step was not going to be a nursing home, so here we go again looking for another assisted living place. We had about a week to come up with a solution.

CHAPTER NINE

ANOTHER MOVE

As we looked around at a few ALC's we hadn't seen before, something caught our eye. As I mentioned in chapter five, a few ALC's had set a section aside for Dementia patients. The word on these places was that the ratio of caregivers to residents was better and they utilized people trained in the care of Dementia patients. This could be just what Mother needed to keep her out of a nursing home.

My wife and I made an appointment to visit a very nice ALC that had a separate Dementia wing. It was totally a lock down situation so residents could not go outside their area. Dementia residents tend to wander off and get lost or hurt. Everything about this place was extremely nice, probably because it was new. It was decorated to the max, which made us wonder about the cost. We took the tour with the director and, since we sort of knew the workings of these places, we told them we would come back with Mother. It was very expensive, at a cost of thirty five hundred dollars per month. We visited two other ALC's that were close to being the same in dealing with people who need assisted care. Both were smaller than the first one and did not have the fancy decor. The pricing of these two was similar at around twenty five hundred dollars per month. We did like the manager at the one place and her approach to Dementia residents, although she did not have a dedicated area specifically for people with Dementia. The manager, Laurie, told us that she had her CNA's devote more time to Dementia residents based on an individual need, but did not have as yet, a specific program. It was nice that she felt this way and that she was conscientious, but we wondered how effective her policy was. We took Mother to the "expensive" place for lunch and while we were there, they gave her a test to see if she needed Dementia care. The test is a standard state test with very simple questions, of which some I believe, are too simple for any one with even just a short-term memory loss. To me, not remembering what was for breakfast or yesterday's weather does not necessarily signify Dementia. Well, Mother did not get a high enough percentage of the questions correct and was determined to be a candidate for the Dementia wing. We really knew this so we were not surprised. Mother did look at all three places, but she would not commit to liking any of them. Time was again running out on us due to Mother having to be out of her current ALC. It really looked as though the first one we visited, the "expensive" one, was going to have to be Mother's new place. It was the only one we had seen or heard of in town that specifically catered to Dementia patients. My wife and I reluctantly filled out the necessary paperwork and paid the non-refundable five hundred-dollar processing fees. Now we had to make arrangements again to have Mother's belongings moved to her new place.

I had sort of led Laurie, manager of the second place, to believe that Mother might like living at her establishment due to the more personal care she supposedly would be given. This was the place without the specific program for Dementia. Since we didn't choose her place, I thought I should call her and tell her not to count on Mother. I told her where Mother was going and she was very understanding wishing her luck in her new place. I contacted the moving company and everything was seemingly in place.

A couple of days went by and I received an unexpected call from Laurie, the manager of the second place that we kind of liked. She said a colleague of hers, Francy, was a marketing director at an ALC that only specializes in Dementia. Another good aspect of this place was that it was only nineteen hundred dollars per month base price. Laurie said she gave Francy my phone number and she would tell her to call me right away. I received an immediate call from Francy and even though it was six p.m., she invited my wife and me out that evening to look over the place. We left right away and arrived there in a half-hour. The place was nice looking from the outside, all on one floor and as I had been told, only about two years old. We met Francy at the front door, which was locked to everyone, since the whole facility was for Dementia residents. The resident's apartments were locked to keep them from wandering into each other's rooms. Everyone was allowed to go anywhere in the facility they desired.

Francy gave us a tour and went over the pricing, staffing ratios and services offered. I liked the CNA to resident ratio, which were six to eight residents to one CNA. We looked at a studio apartment for Mother, which was a step down for her, but we felt since Mother fell in her last one bedroom place, that a studio would lessen her chances of falling. This meant some of her furniture would have to be discarded to be able to furnish her studio without having it too crowded. We decided quickly on this place because it seemed to have satisfied our needs better than any other place. We gave Francy a small refundable deposit to hold a specific apartment for Mother and then set a move in date. Before we left, Francy told us one reason that Laurie had her contact us was that both of them had knowledge that the place where we had put down a deposit had internal problems, causing families to gather together and initiate action. We thanked her for the information. The next item of concern was our five hundred-dollar non-refundable deposit we had given the other place. I called them the next day to get it back, but they said the check had gone to the home office, but they would see if it could be canceled. I did not want to take a chance on them not voiding the check, so my wife stopped payment on the check to make sure it wasn't cashed. We hoped this would take care of the problem so we could concentrate on getting Mother moved to Francy's place.

The movers came to pack Mother's furniture and belongings to move to her new place. My wife and I took a lot of personal items in our car so we could set her up quickly. The loading was fast so we headed out while Mother was again saying goodbye to all that turned out to see her off. During the loading process Mother was sitting in the living room as calm as could be laughing and joking. I told my wife that I wondered if she thought she was going to live with us, even though she had been told about the new place and had been there. As we recall she liked Francy and had a good time there. Little did we know how bad the rest of the day was going to turn out! As we drove up to the place and turned in, Mother said, "What is this place?" I told her as I did on the way out that she was going to live here and that she had visited this place and enjoyed everyone. She said, "Oh no, I'm not living here." We said we would go in and see how things were today, maybe it's a lot nicer than before. As soon as we got in the door Mother was talking to everyone and was seemingly fine. We all went into the office with Francy to fill out the paper work. Mother looked at us and said, "What are you doing, I'm not staying here, I'm leaving." We tried to explain and calm her down, but she walked out of the office on her walker. I asked Francy what were we going to do. The movers were unloading, Mother can't walk unsupervised in a strange place and we had to do the paperwork. Francy brought in the supervising RN, Brenda, and the consensus of opinion was for us to continue signing in, arrange her apartment for tonight and keep out of Mother's site while doing all this. My wife and I decided we had no choice, even though we didn't want it to work this way. Picture this, Mother, ninety-two and on a walker, was in the lobby talking to everyone that would listen saying, "I'm calling the police if I can't get out of here and go home." It was hard to leave her out there without us, but I was hoping Francy and Brenda knew best. My wife and I had to sneak in and out of the place using the side door to bring in her belongings that were in the car, so we could arrange her apartment after the movers left. It took us at least an hour to get everything set so she would have some place that was comfortable to start out in. I asked Francy where Mother was and she said that she was in the lobby talking and had calmed down some. They were introducing Mother to other residents trying to ease her mind. We didn't want to leave, but we had to go so Mother could get used to being there without us. We were very concerned what would happen in the remaining evening. Brenda told us Mother would have something to eat, be looked after and helped to bed later. Brenda said Mother would be checked on every half-hour due to the harsh circumstances she came in under. We were told we could call in at anytime of the night to check on Mother, but it was best if we stayed away for two or three days to let her acclimate herself. I agreed to do this, although it was a hard thing to do, but I did call in later that first night to check on her. I talked to a CNA and was assured everything was fine and Mother was in bed sleeping. Mother probably got more sleep that night than my wife and I.

Over the next three days I kept in close contact with Mother's place to make sure she was all right and if there was anything I could do. The report was that Mother was fine and had actually slept all night long the first night and thereafter. I told them it was her first full night's sleep in a long time without getting out of bed. She was also getting along fine during the day with everyone. I wondered what Mother would do or say whenever my wife and I finally went back to see her?

Evidently all her medicines that we brought over bubble packed were okay and being used. Actually there wasn't much medicine to bring because I had recently had a lot discontinued. Being at a new place, we had to deal with the pharmacy this new ALC deals with. It was a little more expensive, but again you are tied into using their pharmacy. All medicine that is still in force and not discontinued is automatically ordered on a monthly basis. The administration of the medicine is the same as before, whereby only an RN or LPN can give it to the residents.

The day had arrived to go to see Mother for the first time since we left her alone in the lobby. After an attendant let us in the front door, she said that Mother was in her room watching television. My wife and I walked toward her apartment and when we arrived, we decided to unlock the door with our key and peek in and knock at the same time. We did this and Mother, sitting in her chair, looked up and said, "Hey, look who's here!" We were waiting for the bombshell as to why we left her there and why we had not visited in a while. To our surprise Mother was as normal as before and said nothing about where she was or where we had been. She was talkative and seemed in good health. Mother did not remember anything about the episode that took place three days earlier. We spent the rest of the day with her and told her we would see her tomorrow. She did get a little upset with us for leaving, not wanting us to go, but we told her we would see her the next day.

Things were going along pretty well with Mother. We liked the staff a little more than at the other places Mother had been. The RN's and LPN's were my contacts for anything I wanted and they were very accommodating. If I needed more authority, I went to Mary, the director, who was also very willing to help. Generally the CNA staff seemed friendlier and more dedicated to the job than others. I believe that it was due to the location, which was more rural. Most of the staff was local and seemed to have more of a work ethic, with some of the staff having been in the care business quite a few years. A few of the CNA's were sisters and cousins, which I think helped them to work better together. When I watched the staff take care of Mother and the other residents, it appeared as though they really liked each one and had real respect for them.

Soon after Mother moved I found her at her door in a wheelchair, trying to get into her apartment. She had a key, but couldn't use it very well. When she saw me she asked, "How did you know where I was?" I told her I always knew where she was and that she had just moved here. She was afraid so I took her into her apartment and went to investigate the wheelchair and why she was in it. A staff member said Mother just found the chair and started using it. Kathy, the new supervising LPN, said that

Mother wouldn't walk to meals so they put her in the wheelchair to take her to eat. I asked Kathy not to put Mother in a wheelchair and for them to persevere with her walking a little more. Two weeks had passed since the move and Mother was getting along very well. She was sleeping better and going to bed and getting up whenever she wanted, within reason. If she missed breakfast, the CNA's would fix her something to eat from the staff kitchen because Mother did not have any cooking facilities. She had a refrigerator, toaster and coffeepot but did not use them very much. This time we had elected to go with a studio apartment which was a better idea from a "getting around" standpoint. Her overall wellness could be attributed to more liberal sleeping hours, eating intervals more suited to her and just better genuine attention. We thought that we had finally found a place where Mother could be healthier and happier.

One afternoon my wife and I walked into Mother's apartment to find her with her walker at the kitchen sink cleaning up. She was so happy to see us, smiling, laughing and walking, sometimes pushing the walker aside while going around her apartment. We decided to go to the grocery store to get more bottled water and some hearing aid batteries. Mother always liked to push the shopping cart in stores, so we wondered if we could get her to do this now. As we all got in the store I brought a cart over to her and hoped for the best. I took her walker and she walked to the cart and proceeded to go down the aisles. She wanted to buy everything she saw especially cookies and other sweets. Mother looked so well that I ran to the car to get a camera so everyone could see how see was doing.

Mother's new place, as with the others, has a beauty shop that we would make an appointment with every two to four weeks. At this point she was remembering her hair appointments, which made us think her memory was fairly stationary. Mother did have some "moments" in the beauty shops after I would drop her off or after a CNA would take her. Sometimes she would put up such a fuss in the shop that they would take her back to her apartment.

Mother had been in her current apartment for about two months and doing extremely well. She would come to our home, go out to eat and do other errands with my wife and me. Then I got another of those ominous calls that Mother had somehow fallen off her chair. Nothing appeared to have been broken, but her leg that had healed was in pain. I asked Kathy to have her transported to the hospital and we would meet her there. When we arrived Mother was in a good mood waiting for the x-ray results. Everything came back negative this time, but since she had pain, the doctor wanted to observe her overnight in the hospital.

We brought Mother home the next day with her leg in enough pain that she did not want to walk. I had Mother's surgeon review her x-ray for a second opinion and he confirmed that there was no damage to the leg, but it should be sore for a while. Mother was very sleepy and I had to feed her in her room. It was evident she had been given pain pills that left her in this condition. In a couple of days she was back to her old self as far as personality goes.

We decided that therapy should be called back in to help Mother get walking again. She was capable of walking but was afraid due to the soreness, and I guess it did hurt to stand. I thought therapy could do more for her than I could because she would not walk for me. The therapists had some mild success with her walking a few steps using her walker. Her doctor suggested a pain pill that unfortunately had a codeine base, as the one in the hospital, which made Mother very lethargic. The pain in the leg, not wanting to walk and being sleepy frequently was leading Mother not to eat or drink. Again we had to come up with another plan when things change, as they do in the care of older people. We decided to cut the pain pill as much as possible, be more diligent about giving fluids and start a calorie drink such as "Boost" to pick up the slack in nourishment due to poor eating. Also we got her doctor to renew her prescription for the appetite enhancer.

In just a few weeks since her last fall, Mother was not looking good at all. She was becoming dehydrated and I told Kathy this could result in some action such as intravenous feeding at the hospital. Kathy agreed to keep a very close watch on Mother over the next few days, because Mother did not seem to be reacting well to our latest plan.

Kathy called early one morning, just a few days after we had decided to keep a steady vigilance on Mother. She said the eyelids of Mother's eyes had no pink color to them at all and that when her skin was pulled, it did not spring back to shape soon enough, which are good indications of dehydration. I asked Kathy to get her dressed and we would be out to take her to the hospital. When we arrived at Mother's place, she was in her wheelchair with two sweaters on and covered with a blanket, shivering from being cold. We put her in the car and went to the emergency room, once again. The doctors decided to admit her for three days to try to hydrate her with intravenous feedings. Over the next three days Mother developed more color, was not cold anymore and generally felt better. After the third day we took her back to her apartment to start back where she had left off.

Although the leg seemed better, walking appeared to be fading fast. I believe Mother didn't care to walk anymore and had forgotten that she had ever walked with a walker. I would still have her walk in her apartment as much as possible when I was there. Whenever we took Mother anywhere we would have her walk to the car and, if it were to our home, she would have to walk from the car to the house. We would not let her be 100% wheelchair bound.

We discontinued therapy due to her lack of interest and on the therapist's advice. So, Mother's general health at this time was pretty good as we were continuing with the "Boost" drink, the appetite enhancer and pushing fluids. One interesting episode that certainly led to decreased eating for Mother and the other residents was that the food was cold when served. At this particular lunch one day a table mate of Mother's said, " This food is always cold". Well, it really was and it didn't take long to look around and see the problem. I can't believe I didn't notice before, the method they used to serve the food. The food was scooped hot onto each plate one at a time in the kitchen and put on carts. After this was done plate by plate, the carts were pushed into the dining room and each uncovered plate was served individually. The residents seated closest to the kitchen received the hottest food, but from there on the food got cooler and cooler. Having covers over them, like other places, have would have eliminated most of the problem. Of course I went to the director and explained my problem, to which she was most receptive and agreed to modify the serving method.

Mother entered her new place at the end of July and it was now nearing Thanksgiving. There had been a couple of house sponsored parties that Mother had enjoyed, one having a Hawaiian theme where she got to wear her authentic "Moo Moo" that she purchased when she visited Hawaii. We had Mother over for Thanksgiving and had fun going through some old photos trying to bring back some of her memories. She got dressed in her nicest clothes and we had her favorite drink, a whiskey sour, and had a nice time together.

Time was rolling by and Christmas was near. We told Mother that we would celebrate Christmas with her before we went to see my wife's family in Pittsburgh. That was fine with her and she understood the whole situation. Since she has been in this place where more attention is given to Dementia residents, I didn't see the need to go with sitters again while we were away. The time came and we did celebrate Christmas with Mother at our home; then left for Pittsburgh for a week. We were confident of the care she would receive, but we still called her every other day to talk with her and the staff. She was getting along very well and her health remained stable.

When we returned, Mother was happy to see us, remembering that we had been away for Christmas.

She was in good spirits and appeared to be in good health, although her weight had not increased. Over the next few weeks in January, things went along sort of uneventful.

Kathy called one day around the first week of February and said that a flu outbreak had set in and they weren't allowing any visitors and that residents were being confined to their rooms. Food would be taken to each resident and all other care would remain the same. Anyone that needed a doctor would be sent to the hospital so as not to infect other residents. As of now, Mother did not have any signs of the flu. We didn't feel as though we wanted to wait for things to take their course before we checked on Mother, so we went to see her. There was a note on the front door of her place saying they preferred no visitors during this outbreak. We rang the bell anyway and were let in and allowed to go to Mother's room to visit. The staff was letting her stay in bed if she wanted to, but we thought that it was best to have her out of bed. We got some food for her and had lunch together in her room. She seemed to be fine and not affected by any sickness that was going through the place.

A week went by and the flu was over and everyone was back to normal. It was Wednesday February 13th and I had made a doctor's appointment for Mother because she had a slight cough and I wanted to see if there was any problem.

Stewart Nosky

We went to her regular geriatric doctor, a young female who had always seemed interested and competent. During the checkup everything was normal except her blood pressure, which was lower than ever before. I made a comment about it but was told that blood pressure fluctuates like that in older people. Everything checked out fine and there was no problem concerning the cough. We left the office, did some errands, then took Mother for an ice-cream cone. She seemed disinterested that day, especially when she didn't want but one bite of a cone that she normally devours. We went back to her place for a while to talk and left a short time later with her sitting in the dining room. She was with one of her dinner companions dunking a chocolate chip cookie in her coffee and waving goodbye. We were glad the doctor had given her a satisfactory bill of health. This was the evening of the 13th and on the morning of the 15th, I received a call that she had passed away in her sleep.

CHAPTER TEN

A PERSONAL AFTERWORD

After receiving the call, I called my brother to let him know about Mother. My wife and I hurried out to her place to take care of things. She was lying in bed with only her head above the bed covers. Nothing was unusual looking as we checked over the room. We stayed for a little while and then left the room. Mary, the director, had some paperwork for me to sign as the Funeral Director was picking up Mother. After the paperwork we went out in the hallway as she was leaving the building.

We asked Patty, the LPN on duty that morning, exactly what happened. She told us that Mother had gotten up to the bathroom, with a CNA, at 4:30 a.m. and was fine. They were making checks at 6:30 a.m. and a CNA found her not to have any vital signs. Patty, who had not come in yet, was called and she said to start CPR right away and call the fire rescue and HEMSI. CPR was started right away by a CNA but she could not revive Mother. The fire rescue and HEMSI arrived and had the same response. Basically she had passed away in her sleep.

While my wife and I were still in the building, Frances, a CNA that we knew approached us. She was a very reliable older woman that had liked Mother. She asked if we knew what had happened to her, and we said we assumed it to be cardiac arrest. She said she had heard some things and was obviously upset. I asked Frances what she had heard and she said that a night CNA came in and saw Mother in bed with her head back and mouth open. She didn't say that someone gave CPR right then, but at some point someone gave her CPR while she was in bed on a soft surface. Frances said CPR could hurt a person if not given on a hard surface. She did say that this was hearsay, but she did not like some of the CNA's on night shift. Frances also said that five people had recently died there and she was very upset knowing that Mother had just been to her doctor. I told Frances that I would speak to her again.

We took care of what had to be done here at home, then moved on to Pittsburgh, where Mother would be laid to rest. Everything was nicely done and a lot of her family and friends were present, as you would expect. We spent a few days there and then returned home.

I wanted to talk to everyone involved with Mother's death as soon as possible. I located the fire and rescue man, Rusty, and had a discussion with him. Basically he agreed with the story I had already heard, adding that he and the ambulance people, HEMSI, ran an electrical heart test which showed no heartbeat. This is relayed to the hospital medical control that decides whether to go further. Rusty did say that a CNA told him she talked to Mother at about 6:15 a.m. and she said she wasn't feeling well and wished she would pass away. She was then checked at 6:30 a.m. and the rest of the story remains the same. I mentioned to Rusty about the supposed CPR done on Mother while in bed, and he had no comment. He did question why a CNA has to call to get permission to use CPR, but he thought it was probably a rule.

My next interview was with Rhoda, the CNA who was with Mother through most of the ordeal. This gets a little bazaar as we get into it, although different people believe different things. Rhoda put Mother to bed sometime before midnight and said she was in good spirits. Rhoda checked Mother around midnight and took her to the bathroom. She said she was talking, unlike herself, about going to heaven before morning. She said she didn't want to live anymore and would Rhoda stay with her until she went to sleep. After Mother went to sleep, Rhoda went to check on other residents. She came back at 4:00a.m. to take Mother to the bathroom again and Mother started talking about my brother and me and all the good times we had together. Rhoda said Mother also said she saw six angels and her husband and asked Rhoda if she saw them.

Rhoda said Mother was content and sleeping when she left her room at 5:00 a.m.

The story goes on with a CNA, Sherry, who was a supervisor, checking on Mother at 5:15 a.m. and finding no pulse. This is an hour earlier than was first related to me. Well, Rhoda said she couldn't believe it and went in to see and found Mother with a weak pulse and her head and eyes tilted back. She said she kept mother breathing by giving CPR and having someone call the rescue teams. The story remains the same as the rescue people arrive and try to revive Mother. One interesting thing Rhoda volunteered was that because Mother was on a soft surface, she did not try to push too hard on her. Rhoda said that she left and went home after the rescue people were through, because she was so upset.

I had one person to track down and that was Sherry, the CNA supervisor who first discovered Mother. Sherry was no longer working at this facility, so I had to get someone to call her to tell her to call me. Sherry started with how she checked Mother at 4:30 a.m. and she was fine. Rhoda had never mentioned Sherry being involved during the night. Sherry went back to check Mother in about one hour and said she was awake playing with her covers as she tends to do a lot. She went back again at 6:30a.m.and that's when she couldn't find a pulse and ran to get Tammy, a team leader. Tammy, a new person to be involved, according to Sherry, came in with Rhoda who started giving CPR as the other stories go. The rescue team's involvement according to Sherry was the same as stated before by other people. Sherry said she was told not to stay at the facility and left with Rhoda. Other people told her she should stay until the coroner arrived. Sherry says that Mary, the director, was upset with her about some of the things she had done, particularly about the time interval checks on Mother not being correct. She said people started turning against her and she was soon asked to leave. I asked her why they turned on her and she would not or could not give a reason.

Well, that concluded my detective work, but I just had to follow through and find out what happened. The idea to do this may never have occurred to me if Frances had not been suspicious. I'm not sure today what actually happened and I probably never will know. Sometimes too much information is worse than no information. Maybe I'll run into Frances again someday and have a nice chat.

About the Author

Stewart Nosky is a relatively new author having only been a writer of technical procedures manuals for cost engineering and scheduling. He wrote these manuals following specific detailed criteria and from his years of experience. His venture into writing "Dementia" was inspired by his mother, who went through many phases of dementia before the end. Together with his wife, he was able to get through the ordeal, and eventually put his thoughts in book form. The intent was to tell a story that would possibly give people in similar situations some idea of what was ahead.

www.ingramcontent.com/pod-product-compliance
Lightning Source LLC
Chambersburg PA
CBHW051421280526
45785CB00003B/1108

* 9 7 8 1 4 1 0 7 5 5 6 8 1 *